CORPORATE TAX AUDIT SURVIVAL

A View of the IRS Through Corporate Insider Eyes

By Cliff Jernigan
Foreword by Larry Langdon

Olive Hill Lane Press
Woodside, CA

CORPORATE TAX AUDIT SURVIVAL
A View of the IRS Through Corporate Insider Eyes

By Cliff Jernigan
Foreword by Larry Langdon

Published by
Olive Hill Lane Press
2995 Woodside Road, Suite 400
Woodside, CA 94062 USA

ISBN 0-9655769-2-2

WHAT INDUSTRY LEADERS SAY ABOUT THIS BOOK

Former IRS Commissioners

"For every attorney or law firm that counsels corporations or other clients on their tax audits, Cliff Jernigan's new book is a must-read. Its insights and advice about how to deal with the IRS are right on the money. I recommend that you buy it, read it, follow its advice, and keep it close by for easy reference in all of your IRS dealings."

Lawrence B. Gibbs, Commissioner of the Internal Revenue Service, 1986– 1989; member of the law firm of Miller & Chevalier, Washington DC

"Cliff Jernigan has been able to capture in this book the enthusiasm and energy of the new Large and Mid-Size Business Division of the Internal Revenue Service from its inception in 1999 to the present. He also provides very helpful advice for those senior executives considering government service. This is a very useful book for anyone dealing with the corporate community."

Charles O. Rossotti, Commissioner of the Internal Revenue Service, 1997– 2002; co-founder and CEO of American Management Systems, Inc., and Senior Advisor for the Carlyle Group in Washington DC. Author of the best-selling book Many Happy Returns, Harvard Business School Press (2005)

Former International Presidents of the Tax Executives Institute

"Cliff Jernigan has written an insightful overview and history of the first years of the IRS's Large and Mid-Size Business Division. Since I share with him a corporate executive background, as well as a leadership role in LMSB's beginnings, I can vouch for the validity of his observations. I recommend this book to all corporate personnel who deal with the IRS."

Linda B. Burke, President, 1994–1995; former Director of Tax for Alcoa, Inc. and the first Division Counsel for the Large and Mid-Size Business Division of the Internal Revenue Service

"Cliff shows his wide industry experience and insights in this book. I highly recommend it to anyone in the corporate community."

Sol Coffino, President, 1982–1983; Principal and Senior Vice President-Taxes and Acquisition Services, The Fremont Group

"Through his unique perspective, Cliff provides the corporate tax professional with a roadmap to surviving the next corporate tax audit. A simple and concise plan to save your company money."

Lester D. Ezrati, President, 1998–1999; Senior Vice President, Tax, Hewlett-Packard Company

"Cliff has done it again. This book provides valuable insights into the IRS and its relationships with taxpayers. It should prove to be an invaluable tool to tax executives."

Bob Perlman, President, 1992–1993; former Vice President of Tax, Licensing and Customs, Intel Corporation; former Director in the Washington DC National Tax Service Office of PricewaterhouseCoopers LLP

"Cliff Jernigan's experience spans the corporate community, the IRS and the Congress — and he is perceptive and adept on all three. This book includes his candid insights, based on first-hand experience, and is highly informative."

Raymond G Rossi, President, 2003–2004; Director of External Tax Affairs for Intel Corporation

Acknowledgments

I want to thank Larry Langdon, who wrote the foreword to this book, as well as my distinguished endorsers, for their many thoughtful comments to the early drafts of this book.

Thanks also go to Doug Berg, former Senior Industry Advisor for the Natural Resources Group of the Large and Mid-Size Business Division and now at PricewaterhouseCoopers, for his review and many comments, and to Linda Burke, first Division Counsel to the Large and Mid-Size Business Division, for her assistance, especially in writing the chapter on IRS Counsel.

Mike Murphy, former IRS Deputy Commissioner, later Executive Director of the Tax Executives Institute, and presently at the law firm of Sutherland, Asbill & Brennan, was also very helpful with his advice and comments at various stages of the book.

Finally, I would like to give a special thanks to my wife Berdine, who said, "You are not going to write another book, are you?" She has been with me every step of the way for this time-consuming project.

Copy editor *Christine Hopf-Lovette*
Book design and layout *Spot-on Creative*
Book printing *Far Western Graphics*

THANKS FOR THE MEMORIES

I would not have survived my four years at the IRS without the help of the Oakland Headquarters staff of the Communications, Technology and Media Group. I want to give special thanks to Tom Wilson, Frank Ng, JoAnn Bank, Kay Fenton, Frances McGinnis, Kandace Norwood, Ethel McCullough and the rest of the staff.

I also appreciated the advice of legal counsel Jim Clark and Barbara Leonard for making sure that what I wanted to do was consistent with IRS protocol and regulations.

On a day-to-day basis, I could not have survived without the help in my San Jose office of Cliff Hamaishi and Terri Venerable, who made life more manageable by making sure I did not have to wade through a maze of government regulations just to request an expense reimbursement or to file various other required reports.

TABLE OF CONTENTS

Chapter 6

Chapter 7

Chapter 8

FIGURES AND TABLES

About the Author

A California native, Cliff Jernigan holds a bachelor's degree in history, with a minor in English, from the University of Oregon, a law degree (J.D.) from the University of California's Hastings College of the Law, and an advanced tax law degree (LL.M) from New York University School of Law. He is a long-time member of the California Bar Association.

Jernigan has been associated with a New York City international law firm and has held corporate tax counsel positions at Bank of America, Stauffer Chemical Company, and Castle and Cooke (now Dole Foods). From 1979–2001 Jernigan was Director of Taxes and General Tax Counsel and Worldwide Director of Government Affairs at Advanced Micro Devices (AMD). For the period April 2001–April 2005 Jernigan was in the top management of the IRS, serving on the leadership team of the Large and Mid-Size Business Division.

In April 2005, Jernigan founded his own law firm. The firm concentrates in two areas: federal tax audit strategy and representation before the California Legislature and the U.S. Congress. For more information about Mr. Jernigan's law firm, the reader can visit his web site at www.cliffjernigan.com.

Jernigan has been a leader in promoting positive relationships between industry and the IRS. He was a founder and first president of the Santa Clara Valley Chapter of the Tax Executives Institute in 1983, the founder and Executive Director of the Silicon Valley Tax Directors Group from

1980–2001, the Chair of the Tax Committee of the American Electronics Association (1986) and the Chair of the Semiconductor Industry Association Tax Committee (1995–2001).

An accomplished teacher, Jernigan has been a part-time adjunct assistant professor at Golden Gate University over the past 20 years. His classes have included a law school teaching assignment in international taxation and MBA courses on the legal aspects of international business transactions, the impact of government on the high technology community, and government and the legal environment.

This book is the culmination of his broad education and experiences in both the corporate tax community and the Large and Mid-Size Business Division of the IRS. It is a follow-up to his other published books titled *High Tech Survival — The Impact of Government on High Tech and Biotech Companies* (1996) and *Beyond High Tech Survival — Turning Government Policy Into International Profits* (1998), both published by Olive Hill Lane Press.

FOREWORD

Larry Langdon[1]

Cliff Jernigan is very effective in sharing his cross-cultural experiences as a business executive working within the Internal Revenue Service as Senior Industry Advisor for the Large and Mid-Size Business Division (LMSB). In this book, Cliff brings his wisdom and advice to the corporate tax community.

Debbie Nolan and I recruited Cliff to his IRS role in April 2001, prior to LMSB's first anniversary as an operating division. LMSB's history, however, begins with the Revenue Act of 1998. In large measure, the activities of the LMSB reflect the vision of government service held by then-Commissioner Charles Rossotti and the Phase I and Phase II design teams, led by Bobby Scott, Debbie Nolan and David Robison.

I first met Commissioner Rossotti at the October 1998 OECD conference in Ottawa, Canada, where I was the business spokesman on the issue of taxation of electronic commerce. My next conversation with him occurred in early 1999 when he proposed that I join the IRS as the first Commissioner of the LMSB. This was an opportune time for me, since I was "retirement eligible" as an officer at Hewlett-Packard, and I had

---

1 Larry Langdon is a partner and director of global tax services at Mayer, Brown, Rowe and Maw in Palo Alto, California. From 1999–2003, he was the first Commissioner of the Large and Mid-Size Business Division of the Internal Revenue Service. From 1978–1999, he was Vice President, Tax, Licensing & Customs at Hewlett-Packard Company. A co-founder and former president of the Santa Clara Valley Chapter of the Tax Executives Institute, Larry was international president of the Tax Executives Institute during the period 1988–1989. He is a member of the California, Ohio and Michigan Bars.

deployed my tax, export licensing, and customs team between Hewlett-Packard and Agilent as part of the Agilent spin-off.

I met Debbie Nolan in June 1999, and she was subsequently selected as Deputy Commissioner, LMSB. Debbie's appointment marked the beginning of a very exciting business partnership in which I would provide the connection to the external world while she would focus on the internal IRS world. We decided that all of our direct reports would report jointly to the two of us, and we compared the "start up of LMSB" to a start-up business in Silicon Valley.

Selection of the "Team of 38"

On August 25, 1999, Bob Wenzel, Deputy Commissioner of the IRS, administered the oath of office to me at Hewlett-Packard corporate offices, and Bob, Debbie Nolan and I reviewed the appropriate 225 senior executives of the IRS to determine the viable candidates for the 31 career executive positions in LMSB. Debbie and I interviewed over 50 candidates, using "behavior interviewing techniques," to determine the best-qualified. The six "critical pay" positions (five Senior Industry Advisors and the U.S. Competent Authority) to be hired outside the Service took longer to recruit.

Debbie and I also assisted in the recruitment of Linda Burke as Division Operating Counsel and Cindy Mattson as Deputy. Linda and Cindy were part of the Chief Counsel's Office, but, for our operating purposes, they were part of our team, and they were included in all of our team meetings.

Role of Industry and Regional Directors

Before the restructuring of the IRS under the Revenue Act of 1998, the IRS was organized on the basis of four regional commissioners and district directors spread geographically across the country. Each of the district directors was, in large part, thoroughly independent with regard to district strategy *vis à vis* compliance initiatives.

Debbie and I made it very clear that we supported the move to take decision-making down to the appropriate level in field operations. This new structure allowed industry directors to develop strategy for audit coverage and issue resolution on an industry-by-industry basis. At this time, technical advisors were brought in as nationwide coordinators — a move that was to improve tax administration.

Stand-Up of LMSB — June 4, 2000

From an administrative standpoint, the reassignment of all of the cases from a regional structure to one that related more closely to industry required systemic changes and a great deal of coordination. Ultimately, we discovered that it was impossible to assign all of the cases to the particular industry director who had line authority over the case. Accordingly, it was necessary to have a series of cross assignments with the understanding that the industry director could intervene to insure uniform resolution of similar issues in an industry.

Town Hall Meetings

Communicating the role structure and methods of operation, both internally and externally, represented a major challenge. We met this challenge with a series of 18 internal town hall meetings. Over 60% of the LMSB employees met with the new executive team to hear the regional goals and objectives. We also held similar meetings with the external stakeholders. With the help of the Tax Executives Institute (TEI), the American Institute for Certified Public Accountants (AICPA), and the American Bar Association (ABA), these meetings were well received and helped to facilitate the change in management process that was so important for the new organization.

Leadership Meetings

In order to ensure alignment and effective communication, two sets of meetings were established for managers and executives in LMSB. The entire management core, down through territory managers, met for several days annually to hear about current developments and to discuss new compliance initiatives and audit philosophy. In addition, we found that it was important to assemble the LMSB executive "Team of 38" on a semi-annual or quarterly basis to discuss evolving issues. To focus our efforts, we developed detailed strategic initiatives on globalization, issue management, human capital, and corporate tax shelters.

Strategic Initiatives

Globalization

It was clear that the LMSB taxpayers were becoming increasingly global in their operations as U.S.-based companies expanded internationally and foreign-based companies increased investment in the U.S. Carol Dunahoo and Bobby Scott led the efforts to increase globalization training for the executive team at Emory University, and this training cascaded into increased global business education programs for LMSB executives, managers and employees.

Issue Management

Issue management was expected to have the largest long-term impact on the operations of LMSB taxpayers because the opportunity to resolve tax controversies earlier in the dispute resolution process offered major potential savings to both taxpayers and the government.

Several initiatives became the cornerstone of the issue management strategy. These included the pre-filing agreements, the Industry Issue Resolution process, the Limited Issue Focused Examinations program, the Comprehensive Case Resolution process, and the Fast Track Appeals Settlement process. Each of these initiatives is discussed in this book, and all except Comprehensive Case Resolution have had varying degrees of success.

Human Capital

As we examined the demographics of the LMSB work force, we realized that almost 50% of our employees would be eligible for retirement within a few years. This meant that we had a major recruiting challenge on our hands that could not be met with the existing IRS workforce.

Jim O'Malley organized a team to attack this problem, actively recruiting external hires at the grade 13 level. We were pleased to be able to refresh our workforce from a large number of highly experienced and skilled external candidates. Jim also increased the use of remote and computer-based education, allowing a whole series of courses beyond traditional classroom offerings to be made available to the LMSB managers and revenue agents.

Abusive Corporate Tax Shelters

Those of us who came to the IRS from the outside, as well as a cadre of revenue agents who had encountered abusive corporate tax shelters, were determined to move quickly on abuses in the use of corporate tax shelters. Within the Office of Pre-Filing and Technical Guidance, we established the Office of Tax Shelter Analysis. This team, headed by David Harris, analyzed information from the field as well as the disclosures filed at the Service Centers, and worked with the Chief Counsel's Office to focus on the challenge. Their efforts resulted in the publication of a list of abusive corporate tax shelters and the drafting of disclosure initiatives.

The most effective disclosure initiative required taxpayers to disclose all of the documents in connection with abusive transactions, including the names of the promoters and their promotional materials. This enabled the IRS to commence promoter audits through which further information was obtained, allowing additional transactions and a large inventory of abusive transactions to be listed. A number of settlement initiatives were put in place, and LMSB worked closely with the Chief Counsel's Office and Treasury to develop a settlement and litigation strategy.

Liaison Activities

External Stakeholders

A number of groups, including TEI, AICPA, and ABA, helped in the formation of LMSB by providing input to the design teams and advising on certain strategic issues.

Other Operating Divisions and Chief Counsel's Office

In order to coordinate activities across the operating divisions, division commissioners and deputies would meet once a month to talk through issues of coordination, mutual interest and teamwork. This enabled us to better leverage the limited resources within the IRS under the Chief Counsel's office. Richard Skilling and B. John Williams of this office were very supportive of LMSB's efforts in the areas of published guidance and delivering support to field people, particularly with regard to the curtailment of abusive corporate tax shelters. The linkages between LMSB and the various associate offices of Chief Counsel's Office and the Treasury were facilitated by Linda Burke and Cindy Mattson, as well as by Jerry Reese and Frank Ng, who first headed up the Office of Pre-Filing and Technical Guidance.

Treasury and Department of Justice

The Chief Counsel's Office and Treasury established the guidance plan. The operating commissioners provided input, making sure there was good administrative coordination. Key regulation projects that helped rationalize issues in the field included the INDOPCO regulations and the revision of the R&D regulations. Pam Olson and Eric Solomon of the Treasury Department were very helpful, and Treasury supported the request for assistance in developing a list of transactions and disclosure regulations for the abusive tax shelter area. Our colleagues at Justice were very supportive, pursuing summons authority in areas such as promoter audits and helping us develop an effective litigation strategy.

The Large and Mid-Size Business Division has been in operation for over five years. The new compliance and enforcement initiatives have been implemented, yet many corporate taxpayers have not experienced efficient, effective and balanced tax administration. Cliff's book is a primer on how many more taxpayers can be involved in a better way of dealing with LMSB and the IRS generally.

Ten Ways to Increase Your Tax Audit Survival-ability

1. Develop trust and rapport with the IRS team auditing your company.

2. Maintain your credibility at all times.

3. Set aggressive time lines for completion of the audit.

4. Consider using the Joint Audit Planning Process program.

5. Request entry into the Limited Issue Focused Examination (LIFE) program.

6. Use Pre-Filing Agreements where possible.

7. Avail yourself of the Fast Track Appeals Settlement program.

8. Engage the IRS in industry and professional meetings.

9. Know when to engage the IRS for relief.

10. When all else fails, go to the Congress for relief.

Part One:
Joining the Large and Mid-Size Business Division

Chapter 1

INTRODUCTION — REFLECTIONS AND INSIGHTS

I believe this is the first book devoted exclusively to the Large and Mid-Size Business Division (LMSB) of the Internal Revenue Service.

I wanted to write this book to accomplish an important personal objective: to bring an external perspective to the inner workings of LMSB. As a senior level industry executive invited to join the IRS for a maximum four-year employment term, I thought my observations would be unique and valuable to both the taxpayer community and to people within the IRS and other government agencies.

My four years with the IRS were thoroughly enjoyable. I met many wonderful people. Government staffers make sacrifices in terms of compensation and fringe benefits that private sector employees do not have to make, and as one steeped in the perks of the private sector, some of these sacrifices were a little difficult for me.

One part of this book addresses the concerns of senior level industry executives considering government service. I wanted to alert them to the pros and cons of such a decision. Government service can be gratifying, but it can also have its less rewarding features, such as lower pay, greater bureaucracy and more intense oversight.

Another part of the book explores ways in which industry and the IRS can improve relations. When I first joined the IRS, my impression was that both sides were uncomfortable with each other. It was analogous to a seventh grade school dance where the boys would line up on one side of the gym and the girls on the other. The two sides would be reticent about talking to each other. I vowed that I would try to improve relations. After four years, I believe there has been some improvement, but it is only natural for the two sides in a contentious relationship to be somewhat wary of each other.

I was a part of the executive team of the LMSB organization. We called ourselves the "Team of 38." Almost every member of this team was based in the Washington DC IRS headquarters or in industry-specific group headquarters located around the country. I was the exception. I worked "in the field" with a group of about one hundred non-executive IRS personnel that included territory managers, domestic and international team managers and coordinators, analysts, issue technical advisors, economists, engineers, computer audit specialists, employment tax and financial products specialists, and counsel.

It was soon clear to me that the perceptions of IRS personnel in the field can be quite different from the views of executives based in Washington. I noted that there was often strong resistance in the field to accept change proposed by Headquarters. At times, Headquarters was not even aware of the problem, but to an observer sitting just a few feet away from a field agent, the tension was visible.

This vantage point was extremely important. Few IRS executives have the opportunity to examine a situation first-hand both in the field and at Headquarters.

Considerable space in this book is devoted to a discussion of ways that audits can be streamlined to save a company staff time and money. These options have come about as the result of several new IRS initiatives that significantly reduce the audit examination and appeals time for corporate taxpayers.

I also present various options to improve corporate tax positions, including advocacy before the IRS and the Congress. These options offer significant tax savings to taxpayers, and I try to spell out clearly how they can be accessed.

I believe this book will be a useful guide for the corporate tax community and for the accounting and law firms that serve them. Academia, the Congress, the IRS and the U.S. Treasury Department may also find value in my observations.

Chapter 2

STAND-UP: THE HISTORY OF LMSB FROM 1999–PRESENT

Key Topics

History of the LMSB

Over the years, public dissatisfaction with the IRS continued to grow to the point where the U.S. Congress felt compelled to look at ways to improve the public's perception of the organization. Congress responded by passing the IRS Restructuring and Reform Act of 1998. The Act gave the Service a clear direction and new challenge: it must do a better job of meeting the needs of taxpayers. Inherent in this challenge was an obligation to be more responsive to the taxpayer's point of view and to establish an environment of open, honest communication and integrity. This chapter describes the manner in which the IRS has restructured itself to meet the needs of large and medium-sized businesses.

Modernizing a huge organization such as the IRS would not be an easy task.

Charles Rossotti, a successful businessman and information systems expert, was chosen to tackle this tremendous challenge. Immediately upon his appointment as Commissioner of the IRS, Rossotti started to revamp the organization. He embarked on a customer service program modeled after the best practices of private industry. He began the process of integrating the IRS's information systems to enable communication among them. Finally, he created a new, less bureaucratic IRS organization with the goal of enhancing communications between employees and management.

This new, flatter organization has four operating divisions, each with responsibility for serving specific groups of taxpayers (Figure 2-1).

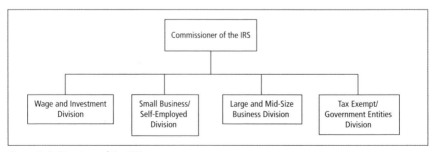

Figure 2-1: Structure of the IRS.

The most important group for the corporate tax community is the Large and Mid-Size Business Division (LMSB).

The provisions of the Act directed Commissioner Rossotti to reorganize LMSB into examination divisions that serve groups of taxpayers with similar needs, effectively eliminating divisions based on geography. Rossotti hired Larry Langdon, head of the Hewlett-Packard Tax Department, to take on this task at the large company level.

Larry Langdon enlisted Deborah (Debbie) Nolan as Deputy Commissioner to help form the LMSB Division in 1999. Nolan was highly regarded within the IRS examination division and brought a wide range of experience to the task.

Over the next few months Langdon and Nolan screened hundreds of applications for key positions in the new organization. In June 2000, the Large and Mid-Size Business Division officially debuted in what was called the "stand-up" of the LMSB.

LMSB Structure

The LMSB was divided into five industry operating groups: Financial Services, based in Manhattan; Natural Resources and Construction, based in Houston; Retailers, Food, Pharmaceutical and Healthcare, based in Chicago; Heavy Manufacturing and Transportation, based in Iselin, New Jersey; and Communications, Technology and Media, based in Oakland, California.

The initial industry directors represented some of the brightest and most competent career employees in the Service.

Dave Robison was chosen for Financial Services. He has since moved on to head up IRS Appeals. Bobby Scott was asked to head up Natural Resources and Construction. Bob Brazzil was appointed to head up Retailers, Food, Pharmaceutical and Healthcare, serving in this position until the middle of 2004. He now has a top executive position with Deloitte and Touche.

Tom Smith was put at the helm of Heavy Manufacturing and Transportation, a position he held until the end of 2002. Tom Wilson was charged with the Communications, Technology and Media Group, which he led until June of 2004. Both Tom Smith and Tom Wilson have since taken top executive positions with PricewaterhouseCoopers.

The five industry groups can be broken down into subgroups as follows:

Financial Services	Retailers, Food, Pharmaceuticals, and Healthcare	Natural Resources and Construction	Heavy Manufacturing and Transportation	Communications, Technology and Media
• Financial Products • Life, Property and Casualty • Commercial Banking	• Agriculture • Biotech • Food & Beverage • Healthcare • Pharmaceutical • Retail	• Chemicals • Construction • Environmental • Forest Products • Mining • Petroleum • Utilities	• Aerospace • Air Transportation • Automotive • Railroads • Shipping • Trucking	• Cable • Movies • Music Recording • Gaming • Publishing • High Technology • Telecommunications • Sports

Table 2-1: IRS Sub-groups.

LMSB Supporting Structure

Support staff for the five industry operating groups included financial products specialists, computer audit specialists, economists, engineers, and employment tax specialists. They reported to Keith Jones, head of the Field Specialist Directorate.

An elite headquarters team reported to Langdon and Nolan. Jim O'Malley headed up finance and human resources; Susan Linden handled communications and liaison; Jerry Reese and Frank Ng formed the Pre-Filing and Technical Guidance function; and Joanne Johnson-Shaw was in charge of Equal Employment Opportunity.

Carol Dunahoo, formerly of PricewaterhouseCoopers, joined Elvin Hedgpeth of the IRS to make up the international team and Competent Authority Office; and Linda Burke, formerly the tax director at Alcoa Corporation, came in to serve as Counsel for LMSB. Paul Witte was chosen as the first Executive Assistant to Langdon and Nolan to keep track of everyone and everything of importance within LMSB.

Other important roles at Headquarters were positions in strategy, research and program planning, quality control, information systems, and e-commerce.

The industry directors and headquarters team then began to fill out their organizations with even more talented people. At "stand-up," LMSB numbered about 6,500 employees out of a total IRS headcount of 100,000 employees.

Initially LMSB had jurisdiction over companies with five million dollars in assets, an amount that was later changed to ten million dollars. (This perception of size in terms of assets was awkward for me because the private sector generally uses sales as the measure of company size.) The companies included in LMSB are primarily corporations, but they could also be partnerships, trusts, and even individuals.

Within each industry group were directors of field operations (DFOs) representing the eastern and western parts of the country. For example, in the Natural Resources and Construction Group, there was a DFO East and a DFO West. These DFOs each had about five territory managers reporting to them. The territory managers had about five team managers, and these managers each supervised several team coordinators who were responsible for handling the day-to-day audits of individual companies.

Senior Industry Advisors

Complementing the LMSB organization was a new category of LMSB executive: the Senior Industry Advisor. These were Treasury Department appointees, of which I was one. We reported to the Industry Directors.

There were five of us. Doug Berg was the first to be hired. He left BP to join Natural Resources and Construction. Paul Claytor was next. He had a long banking career plus a career at PricewaterhouseCoopers before joining Financial Services. Kurt Meier soon followed at Retailers, Food, Pharmaceutical and Healthcare. Meier had a long career at Morton International and Ernst & Young. I came next as the Senior Industry Advisor for the Communications, Technology and Media Group. Prior to the Service, I had been with Advanced Micro Devices. Bob Adams was the last to arrive, joining Heavy Manufacturing from Nortel Networks.

All of the Senior Industry Advisors joined the IRS under a special legislative designation: "critical pay" employee. The Revenue Act of 1998 authorized a maximum of 40 "critical pay" employees in senior-level management and technical positions at any one time.

The Act provided that the pay structure for employees in this category would be closer to a private industry wage, and could be paid to those individuals who possessed skills considered critical to the IRS's successful execution of its restructuring tasks. Under the Act, a "critical pay" employee could not be employed for a term exceeding four years, and the "critical pay" program in the Act was to run for the fixed term of 1998 to 2008.

The organization chart for LMSB by major position is shown below:

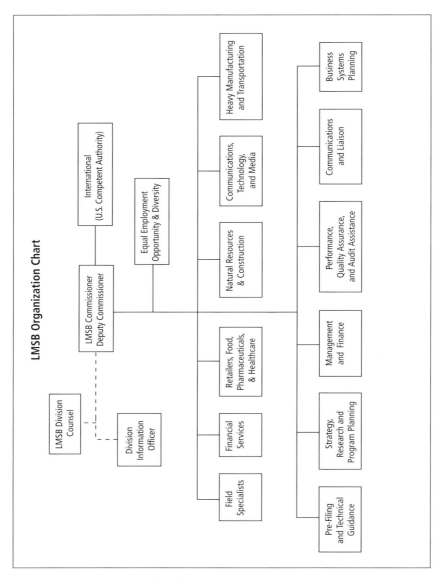

Figure 2-2: LMSB Organization Chart by Major Position.

LMSB Patriots

The initial LMSB employees were a remarkable group of individuals. I think of them as "patriots." Sixty-hour work weeks were not unusual, but no one complained. They understood their assignments and accomplished their tasks in high spirits.

Larry Langdon commuted each week from his home in Northern California to his Washington office to attend 8:00 AM Monday morning meetings with Charles Rossotti. On Friday afternoon he would fly back to California. On Sunday afternoon he would repeat the drill, paying for his own travel, his Washington housing, and his meals. Beyond that, he worked 12-hour days.

Debbie Nolan joined Langdon in this grueling routine as they set up and addressed issue after issue of the new organization. Linda Burke, who commuted from Pittsburgh, was also part of this close-knit team. She, too, paid for her own travel and Washington living expenses.

Many of the industry directors would fly into town to address issues as a team. Some of them commuted almost weekly.

LMSB Management Team in Action

Langdon and Nolan ran a very business-like operation. It was almost corporate in its nature.

We called ourselves the "Team of 38," and at management meetings we would discuss the performance of the various operating groups. We reviewed the number of cases that were closing and what we would need to do to close more, how long audits were taking, why they were taking so long, and what impediments needed to be overcome. We looked at ways to reduce audit time and Service resources, and our team worked on taxpayer initiatives to reduce audit burden on taxpayers and the Service. We also looked at succession planning, since many of our senior employees were nearing retirement age.

The "Team of 38" tried to work "smart" and in a proactive, pragmatic manner.

LMSB in Transition

Much of the success of the LMSB can be attributed to the hard work of these early "patriots."

Many members of the original team have moved on. Larry Langdon left in June of 2003 to join the law firm of Mayer Brown Rowe and Maw. Debbie Nolan was promoted to replace him as LMSB Commissioner. Bruce Unger was brought in as a "critical pay" employee to replace her as Deputy Commissioner.

Many of the external hires, including Linda Burke, Carol Dunahoo, and most of the Senior Industry Advisors have left.

Several of the original Industry Directors have also moved on. Other outstanding individuals came in to fill the Industry Director openings. Paul DeNard is Industry Director of Financial Services; Henry Singleton is Industry Director at Retailers, Food, Pharmaceutical and Healthcare; John Petrella is Industry Director of Heavy Manufacturing and Transportation; and Frank Ng is Industry Director of Communications, Technology and Media.

LMSB Report Card: Successes and Challenges

The taxpayer community has been very receptive to the LMSB organization and the areas of specialization it has brought. Large and medium-size businesses are more satisfied with the IRS than ever before. IRS employees also like this new organization, as substantiated by employee surveys.

Since LMSB's establishment, a number of programs have been initiated to significantly reduce the burden on taxpayers. These programs were created to make the audit run more smoothly, to require less taxpayer financial and human resources, to decrease the amount of time spent on the audit by the taxpayer, and to conclude the audit more quickly. They were also designed to reduce IRS audit resource time and expense, enabling the IRS to audit more taxpayers.

A number of these programs have yielded amazing results and newer ones are showing good promise.

I will cover these programs in much greater detail in Chapter Seven, but I think it is worthwhile to briefly mention some of them here.

1. Pre-Filing Agreements (PFAs)

2. Industry Issue Resolution Agreements (IIRs)

3. Limited Issue Focused Examinations (LIFE)

4. Fast Track Appeals

5. Joint Audit Planning Process

6. Schedule M-3 to the Form 1120

7. Compliance Assurance Process (CAP)

8. Corporate e-file

LMSB has had many challenges, the most important of which may have been the proliferation of abusive tax avoidance shelters that started to appear in the late 1990s. This pervasive phenomenon has, for the most part, been fought successfully, but it required significant financial and manpower resources.

Larry Langdon and Debbie Nolan were very skillful in dealing with abusive tax avoidance shelters through a variety of strategies. They quickly established the Office of Tax Shelter Analysis (OTSA) to help detect abusive shelters. By making shelter activity one of the highest IRS priorities, they focused significant financial and manpower attention to the issue. They required taxpayers to disclose tax shelter transactions on their tax returns and put together settlement initiative programs for different types of shelters. In addition, they aggressively pursued shelter promoters, working with the Chief Counsel's Office to identify the most egregious cases for challenge in court.

Today LMSB appears to be gaining the upper hand on new abusive tax shelter activities, and some companies, firms and individuals are being ordered to pay back-taxes, plus interest and penalties, for their involvement in these shelters.

Another major challenge for LMSB is its aging work force. About one-third of the LMSB staff is eligible to retire, and many employees have already started to leave. The prospect of losing such a large number of people is not good for the Service or the companies they audit. The Service will be losing a strong knowledge base. At the same time, the companies will lose the benefit of agents who know their businesses and their tax issues.

Beginning in 2003, LMSB embarked on a major hiring campaign. As federal hiring dollars became available, they started to replace some of the retiring agents. Overall, however, LMSB is still down in its headcount from the 6,500 at "stand-up." Nevertheless, I believe that the organization, with its strong leadership and motivated employees, will rise to this and other challenges.

Chapter 3

My Move to the Dark Side

Key Topics

In April 2001, I left private industry and moved to the dark side. I joined the Large and Mid-Size Business Division (LMSB) of the IRS.

The phrase "moving to the dark side" would normally have the negative connotations of joining the enemy or siding with the enemy. In the language of the tax community, however, this is not the case. The words are used in a more lighthearted, frivolous, joking manner of banter among friends.

When I joined the IRS, my Silicon Valley tax community friends accused me of joining the dark side. When Larry Langdon left the IRS to join Mayer Brown Rowe and Maw, Cindy Mattson, formerly Division Counsel for LMSB, joked with him about leaving the IRS to go to the dark side with a law firm that had been one of the most able trial firms she had faced in the U.S. Tax Court. And when Dave Robison left LMSB Financial Services Division to join Appeals as Chief, Appeals, he was kidded by his former colleagues for going over to the dark side because of the friendly rivalry between the examination side and the appeals side.

Before the IRS

As I noted earlier, Larry Langdon left the tax department of Hewlett-Packard to start up the LMSB organization.

Langdon and I had been colleagues for about 20 years. We first met when I was the Tax Director at Advanced Micro Devices and he was the Tax Director of Hewlett-Packard. Both companies are located in Northern California's Silicon Valley.

The two of us had been active in furthering the tax interests of the Valley. We put on educational seminars to train our staffs and the staffs of other local company tax professionals. We generated interest among our colleagues to advance tax regulatory and legislative proposals at the federal and California levels. We were co-founders of the Santa Clara Valley Tax Executives Institute. And we were both keenly aware of the impact U.S. tax and trade laws could have on the competitiveness of our companies. We knew we had to engage and educate government officials about the problems we faced.

I was proud of Larry Langdon when he decided to give up his prestigious job at Hewlett-Packard to join the start-up phase of the LMSB organization. He was the first executive from the Silicon Valley tax community to do so. When he told me about the Senior Industry Advisor position for the Communications, Technology and Media Group, I felt that I too should embark on public service as a way to give some West Coast help to my friend and colleague and to further good tax administration. I was honored to be selected for the position.

It was not easy for me to leave my job at Advanced Micro Devices for a senior level government position with only a fixed term of four years. It was risky at best. After four years, what would happen to me? Would I find another job as good as my job at Advanced Micro Devices?

Applying for the Job

The process of applying for a senior level government position was an experience that I would like to share with others from the private sector. Like me, many executives have migrated from the private sector into top level government jobs without knowing first hand what to expect. *Moving from the private sector to the government sector is a decision not to be taken lightly.*

For starters, you will give up your personal and financial privacy. You will most likely earn a smaller compensation package for the term of your government employment, with less vacation time, less medical insurance and no dental benefits, and your employment could trigger income from the exercise of various compensation and stock option plans that could significantly increase your federal and state income tax liabilities in the year of your termination of employment. *Someone going from the private sector to the government sector at a senior level must consider these consequences before making the move.*

Here are the steps that were involved when I applied for this senior government position:

1. Fill out a long job application form.

2. Visit the local police department to be fingerprinted.

3. List all the countries visited, with the dates of entry and departure for the past ten years. This was difficult for me since I had traveled to about 40 countries during this period and it was not always easy to remember my itineraries with this kind of precision. Because I believed this requirement related to possible foreign government subversive activities, I compiled this list with trepidation, fearing that an omission would be viewed as deliberate.

4. List all schools attended (with degrees) back to junior high school, and provide names, addresses and telephone numbers of acquaintances.

5. Prepare an income and assets financial disclosure (which is now subject to public inspection under the Freedom of Information Act Disclosure Rules).

6. List names of employers and immediate supervisors.

7. Provide the names of three personal references.

8. Sign statements that I was an American citizen and that I would uphold and defend the United States. Also sign statements that I had not been convicted of a misdemeanor or felony, or that I was not a member of the Communist Party or other subversive organization.

9. Submit to a background check as to my moral and ethical character. In this regard, Treasury Agents interviewed several people in my neighborhood by showing up unannounced and asking them about me.

Leaving the Private Sector

Once approved, I was still at risk of not being hired by the IRS. Sometimes a complete background check can take up to one year, and if a problem arises, the federal government can terminate you at this later time. At this point, you will not have a job, either with the federal government or the private sector, assuming your private sector employer has already replaced you.

When you enter government service, you will need to sever all financial ties with your private sector employer. This means exercising stock options and triggering other compensation plans. The gains in one year can result in a large federal and state tax bill. 401(k) plans may continue to be managed by the employer, or they can be transferred to an Individual Retirement Account (IRA). I left my 401(k) plan at Advanced Micro Devices for about two years, but after this time I had my local bank put it in an IRA for me.

No promises of employment with your private employer after the federal term ends can be made. The rationale is that the employee must not appear to have a conflict of interest with respect to his past employer or his past industry group.

If you were accustomed to an expense account, you will need to break this habit. There are no expense accounts. You will also need to become accustomed to flying in coach class and staying in lower- to mid-level hotels.

Reality Lessons

I will be the first to admit that it was hard for me to adapt to the government system. I missed the corporate expense account. I never stayed within the government *per diem* meal allowances ($40–50 per day). I usually doubled these allowances on trips and bore the extra expenses personally.

When you join the government at a senior level, the reality is that you should expect to spend a substantial amount of your own money in the job. This is public service, and you are just giving back to the public.

Tax Audits

As part of the IRS hiring process, the government checks to see if you have filed all of your tax returns, and on time. Not doing so could be cause for rejection.

The IRS audits new hires and periodically carries out audits of its own employees to make sure their conduct is ethical. As I have indicated, new hires at the senior level may have triggered a substantial tax bill in the year of hiring due to the requirement that they exercise company stock options and cash out deferred compensation plans. Every extra dollar found on an audit would generate tax at potentially a very high marginal tax rate.

IRS employees joke that the reason the IRS does not audit more of the general public is that its employees are always being audited first, leaving few resources left to carry out other audits. It does seem ironic to me that the IRS spends so much of its resources investigating its own employees when so many of the general public have returns that could generate much more revenue for the government.

Final Observations

As you can see, there are many pros and cons to undertaking government service, especially with the IRS. I have personally enjoyed the experience, and I am happy to have committed a small part of my life to this endeavor.

Chapter 4

I am the CTM SIA from the San Jose POD — I am from Mars

Key Topics

Most individuals who move from the private sector to the public sector have an agenda they want to accomplish during their public term. I was no different.

Prior to my term with the IRS, I spent over 20 years engaging members of the U.S. Congress and their staffs on a variety of tax and other policy issues. I noticed that most of them came to Washington with clear personal agendas.

Some felt that government was too intrusive, and they wanted to lessen its impact on our lives. Others felt just the opposite. Some came to further a social cause. Some came to help create high-paying U.S. jobs and increase U.S. competitiveness around the world. Some wanted to make government processes run more efficiently.

I hoped to pursue four main agenda items:

1. *Improve relations between industry and the IRS.*

2. *Reduce the audit time and cost burden for industry and the IRS.*

3. *Help U.S. industry become more competitive.*

4. *Introduce private industry efficiency to the IRS.*

Throughout the remaining chapters of this book, I will make observations and reflections relating to this agenda. With respect to items 1 and 2, I believe I was part of a success story. I found the going a little harder for items 3 and 4.

The title of this chapter, "I am the CTM SIA from the San Jose POD — I am from Mars," summarizes how ill-prepared I was to join the IRS.

Even though I had years of experience dealing with the U.S. Congress and various regulatory agencies, including the U.S. Department of the Treasury and the IRS, I had always engaged them as an industry representative. To change sides was to enter a whole new world.

My first 30 days on the job were a challenge. I was met with suspicion, and I had trouble with government acronyms, Big Brother warnings, and an unfamiliar environment.

Spy/Traitor/ Disbelief

When I showed up for work my first day at my San Jose office, I was met by a very nice group of IRS employees. I could tell they wondered what a corporate person was doing in their midst. They were friendly, but in a decidedly reserved way. I sensed some of them thought of me as a corporate spy.

I was joining the Service as the highest ranking IRS employee in the San Jose region. The person designated as the Commissioner's Representative for my building gave me a pass to be able to enter into the secured office areas. I saw file cabinets full of confidential corporate taxpayer information. For someone who had spent most of his career opposing the IRS, it seemed strange being here. I felt like the fox that was being asked to guard the hen house.

Just a few miles away, my former corporate tax colleagues were talking about me, wondering if I had become a traitor among them. Would I be turning over the secrets of the corporate community? Would I be someone they would want to talk to again? Frankly, I had been out of the corporate tax department world for several years at this time and was hardly in a position to give away corporate tax department secrets. Nonetheless, the tax community was concerned.

Closer to home, my neighbors were in shocked disbelief. The IRS is not popular in my hometown. They could not believe I had joined an agency so disliked. Many of my friends became uneasy when I told them I had joined the IRS. Because of this universal response, I would generally refrain from telling neighbors and others that I was with the IRS. If asked, I would say I was with the Treasury Department on an assignment to improve government efficiency. This story had a positive ring with them. I later learned that many IRS agents tell their neighbors and social acquaintances the same story.

Acronymphobia

The IRS is an agency that thrives on the use of acronyms. In fact, acronyms flourish to their greatest heights at the Large and Mid-Size Business

Division (LMSB) headquarters in the Mint Building in Washington DC, where "Mintspeak" crops up in every discussion.

In one of my first meetings, I sat among several IRS career employees in the Mint Building. The discussion leader started by saying that we were meeting on the "ABC issue for the DEF area of the GHI problem." I raised my hand and said, "Excuse me, would you mind telling me what the 'ABC issue for the DEF area of the GHI problem' is?" The leader courteously explained the three acronyms to me while the others in the room squirmed in their chairs. I thanked him.

The leader went on. "The GHI problem has a connection to the JKL and MNO and PQR problems, which we need to solve PDQ." I raised my hand again and said, "Excuse me, would you mind telling me what 'JKL' and 'MNO' and 'PQR' stand for? And what is 'PDQ'?" The leader explained the acronyms, and the old-timers rolled their eyes.

I looked at my watch and realized I had taken up about a quarter of the time scheduled for the meeting.

The leader went on to talk about "STUV" and "WXYZ" issues, but I did not raise my hand again. I might as well have been from Mars. A few days later, though, I was able to turn the tables during introductions at another IRS group meeting. When my turn came, I introduced myself as the "CTM SIA from the San Jose POD."

Everyone in the room knew that "CTM" stood for Communications, Technology and Media. They also knew that "POD" stood for post of duty (a military term frequently used in the IRS). However, they did not know what "SIA" stood for.

They were perplexed. Here was an acronym that they could not decipher. I explained that "SIA" stood for Senior Industry Advisor. They were relieved. They could now add a new acronym to their list.

Debbie Nolan, then Deputy Commissioner of LMSB and now Commissioner, gave a speech at an LMSB managers' meeting during my first few months on the job. When it was over she approached me and asked me how I liked the speech. She was grinning.

I replied that I thought it was her usual great speech.

She asked, "Did you notice anything different?"

"I'm not sure," I responded.

She told me that she had avoided all acronyms because she wanted to be certain that I understood her message.

I appreciated her efforts to go beyond "Mintspeak" in her remarks.

While I have learned the meanings of many IRS acronyms, some still leave me in the dark. But I am not alone. Others, too, are overwhelmed by the prospect of sitting through entire meetings that might as well be conducted in a foreign language.

Big Brother

When I first engaged the IRS voice messaging system, I was stunned by the message: "Welcome to the IRS voice messaging system. Unauthorized use of this facility could result in civil and criminal penalties." After this admonition, I was almost afraid to use the IRS phone system.

A few days later I received an email message warning me that I could be disciplined if I did not pay my government credit card bill on time. I thought, "Am I working with a bunch of deadbeats?"

Shortly thereafter I received a sternly-worded message telling me there would be severe consequences, including possible termination of employment, if I incurred estimated tax payment penalties for underpayment of estimated taxes or if I made a mistake on my federal income tax return. I thought, "Am I working with a bunch of tax cheats?"

I considered the references to late payments of credit card bills and tax filing penalties.

Why would IRS employees be receiving these messages? Was I not working with some of the most honorable people in America?

I concluded that the messages were ill-advised and would never have been sent by management in the private sector. Messages like these can only breed hurt feelings and damage morale. To me, the messages are insulting, and I believe the practice should be eliminated.

The System

One of my first IRS assignments was to co-manage a project associated with updating the corporate tax return filing system.

Together with another LMSB executive, I met with a group of IRS employees who had been detailed to a design team for this purpose. An outside consulting firm had been hired to assist the IRS team.

The design team and outside consultant had been discussing options for several weeks. Every wall of the meeting room was plastered with large sheets of paper listing the pros and cons of the project. I asked if they had arrived at any conclusions, and they said they had gotten so mired down in the project details that they were having trouble making any recommendations.

The group asked us to review a report that they were writing to management. We suggested they compose an executive summary to the document in order to help crystallize their thinking. They went back to work and returned with a ten-page executive summary for a 50-page report. Furthermore, the report contained no conclusions. They simply had not been able to identify the major issues.

My associate and I helped them to synthesize their findings into a three-page executive summary, a process that helped them see where the project was going.

Sadly, this design team exercise was typical of my experience with many Service projects. A lot of smart people are expending a tremendous amount of effort without resolving the problems to which they have been assigned. I think the problem is due to a lack of strong leadership during the design team process. Most of the process seems to be consensual, and the attempt to achieve consensus makes it difficult to maintain focus on the end result.

I have one final observation from my first 30 days at the IRS. I had been asked to participate in a team exercise with the other Senior Industry Advisors dealing with an international problem. We all traveled to Washington for a two and one-half day meeting. Facilitators are commonly used in the IRS to help lead discussions, and one had been brought in from the Midwest to help us organize our thoughts.

The meeting might have been concluded in about a day, but because it was scheduled to last two and one-half days, we all had to stay for the entire time. I believe that often too little attention is given to the dollar value of the time that is wasted by requiring meetings to last longer than necessary.

After my first 30 days I became more comfortable with the IRS way of doing things. In truth, my background with industry, especially the 22 years I spent with the very entrepreneurial and free-spirited high-technology sector, never permitted me to be fully at ease with many IRS practices.

I am from Mars

Because of my experiences in the private sector, I sometimes had difficulty fitting into the IRS fabric.

One example of this involved the high-profile debate about whether stock options should be expensed for financial statement purposes. This issue was extraordinarily intense during the 2003–2004 time period, with the Financial Accounting Standards Board (FASB) arguing that stock options should be reflected as an expense on the financial statements while industry argued that they should be reflected as an item on the balance sheet. Most employees in the high-technology sector agreed that they should be reflected as an item on the balance sheet, and I strongly supported the high-technology position.

This topic has no bearing on the filing of a corporate tax return. For tax return purposes, stock option exercises usually are treated as an income tax expense.

My colleagues in the IRS often would argue about this issue over lunch or at other meetings. Almost universally they would take the position that stock options should be treated as an expense for financial statement purposes. I would counter that, in all of my experiences in the high-technology area, it was better not to make this change. They would smile at me (some would glare) as if I did not know what I was talking about. It would have been a futile exercise to try to persuade them otherwise. I would have been like the lone Republican in the House of Representatives trying to persuade the 434 Democrats in that body that they were wrong on an issue. Conversations like these made it clear to me that I might as well be from Mars.

Another time, I was engaged in a discussion about depreciation of telecommunication equipment. It seemed apparent to me that the equipment at issue was similar to high-technology equipment that, by statute, has a depreciation period of five years. At this point, telecommunication equipment was not clearly covered by statute, and the IRS contention was that the equipment had a ten-year life.

I argued that depreciation is merely a timing issue, meaning that it is just a cash flow issue for the government and does not result in lost taxes. On the other hand, the benefit of faster cash flow through faster depreciation means a lot to capital-intensive telecommunications companies.

I also felt that a ten-year life was not competitive relative to depreciation programs for telecommunications companies in other countries. My IRS colleagues had the power to help U.S. international competitiveness if they would agree to five-year depreciation.

They paid lip-service to me but finally chose to apply the ten-year life. Clearly they had decided that I was from some other planet.

While I may indeed have come from Mars, I believe that some of my thinking, and my deportment, may have had an influence on the IRS executive team. Toward the end of my term, I found that they listened to me more often. The meetings seemed to be shorter and more to the point. And I noticed that they sought my advice more frequently.

Chapter 5

THE SECRET SOCIETY

Key Topics

To many people outside of government, the IRS is a secret society that is inaccessible to ordinary citizens. I felt the same way.

IRS activities are indeed kept very private. An IRS building houses confidential taxpayer information within a closed area, and visitors cannot simply walk in and visit the staff. Except for taxpayer assistance areas that are easily accessible, every floor is a secured space that requires special permission for entrance.

Behind the Closed and Secured Doors

Who are the people behind these closed and secured doors?

Most IRS employees have accounting and finance backgrounds. Some have been trained in computer science and information systems. Others are economists and engineers. Some are lawyers. Many are clerical employees.

They joined the IRS for various reasons. Some wanted to do government service. Others, particularly lawyers, wanted government experience before taking jobs in the private sector. In some cases, working for the IRS was a family tradition.

IRS employees cite the risk of losing a job in the private sector as one of the compelling reasons for choosing to work for the government. They like the security the IRS offers.

Characteristics of IRS Employees

Believe it or not, most IRS employees have a good sense of humor. While they must maintain a serious public demeanor, they can be just as crazy in private as my friends in the corporate world. They drink, play practical jokes, and like to have a good time.

They stay at one job for a long time. Most of the IRS employees I know have been with the Service for 15–35 years. They seem to have a level of commitment to their government employer that I have not experienced in the private sector.

My impression, which may be a gross generalization, is that their politics tend to be oriented more to the social causes and programs identified with the Democratic Party than to the conservative causes identified with the Republican Party.

I think of most IRS employees as idealistic. They want to do the right thing. They believe that it is one's patriotic duty to pay his or her fair share of taxes to support the government. They are also fair-minded. In my experience, they generally give the taxpayer the benefit of the doubt.

While they do not appear to be driven by the need to make a lot of money, they are looking for financial security. They do not need to live in luxury. With the exception of some of the top executives, most IRS employees prefer a well-defined work routine of about 40 hours a week. They want to have a good home/work balance, and have time for family activities. They are not workaholics; many are happy to take advantage of the flexible hours that government service offers.

It is not uncommon for IRS employees to date and marry their colleagues. They joked about how difficult it was to date someone on the outside once they revealed that they worked for the IRS.

Salaries at the IRS are often lower than the private sector. The incentive, however, is a pension at retirement that might equal two-thirds or three-fourths of the yearly average of their last few years of annual earnings. This is a benefit many in the private sector do not have.

On the other hand, living costs can be a challenge for government employees, especially in some of the high cost-of-living areas where IRS facilities are located. It is not uncommon for many IRS employees to search for affordable housing at great distances from their jobs. Some of these employees commute up to two hours each way. This is especially true in the San Francisco Bay Area, where employees might live in Sacramento or Stockton and commute 80–100 miles to San Francisco, Oakland or San Jose. Such long commutes are also common in the New York City Metropolitan Area and the Washington DC-Baltimore area.

I have talked to employees in San Jose who go through the following routine: they catch a train or van pool at 4:30 AM to arrive at their job site at 6:30 AM, work until 3:30 PM and get back on the train or van pool at 4:00 PM to arrive home at 6:00 PM. Some do this every day. Others do this twice a week and stay at the job location with friends for two or three nights.

IRS employees like coffee. I have noticed this especially among IRS counsel employees. They tend to favor Starbucks. They will walk for blocks to buy their favorite brew.

People of Pride

IRS employees are a proud group. They are cohesive. They stick together and defend each other. There is a good *esprit de corps* in the Service.

This strong bond among IRS employees is admirable, but it does not always work to the advantage of the Service. I detected resentment against individuals who offered legitimate criticisms of IRS policies and procedures. In fact, I received glowering looks during a few meetings when I offered what I believed were practical suggestions. There was a noticeable "circling of the wagons" in defense of what they believed was unfair criticism.

The IRS receives so much criticism that it often has difficulty separating constructive suggestions from mean-spirited censure. They are not used to having people like me come into their organization from the outside and offer suggestions as if I were one of them.

No one likes to pay taxes. In the face of this, it is easy to see how IRS employees develop a siege mentality of toughness against outside threats and insults. Nevertheless, the government depends on IRS auditors to carry out an important job. Sadly, it is often a thankless task to collect revenues that help run the country.

Dennis McCarthy, a retired IRS LMSB manager, sent me this lament, penned in fine calligraphy. Written by an anonymous IRS employee, it captures some of the pride and spirit of the Service.

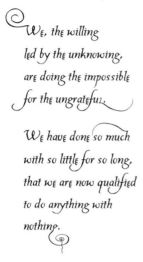

We, the willing
led by the unknowing,
are doing the impossible
for the ungrateful.

We have done so much
with so little for so long,
that we are now qualified
to do anything with
nothing.

Caring People

IRS employees are caring people. They are idealistic. The IRS workforce has great continuity, and people stay together for years. In a sense, the IRS is a big family. When one of them becomes severely ill, it is not uncommon for their colleagues to donate vacation time in order to extend the employee's sick days.

IRS employees hold potluck lunches for holiday events, baby showers, promotions, and retirements. They also socialize among themselves, typically at after work get-togethers and events, such as monthly golf tournaments or social gatherings at museums.

I am impressed by the way IRS management steps forward to personally fund occasional employee events. In the private sector, the company would have a budget for these activities. Management would be reimbursed when it incurred out-of pocket expenses. The government does not work this way. It is not uncommon for individual IRS managers to spend hundreds of dollars of their own money each year to fund employee events.

The Secret Society Exposed

When I joined the IRS, I made the comment that I was going to learn things about an organization that most people did not know. My new colleagues responded that the IRS had nothing to hide. I told them I thought it was a secret society because the general public did not know how the agency operated.

At the end of my four-year term, my IRS colleagues suggested to me that I had received four years of valuable training and obtained insights that most people never get; I had learned about the inner workings of the IRS. I agreed. It was a valuable and rather unique experience.

I learned about the temperaments, prejudices, preconceived notions, and political views of IRS employees that do not appear in published guidance of any form, but which certainly have a bearing on a tax outcome.

IRS employees are not unlike the rest of us. They want to make society better. They are good citizens in their communities. They are caring. They are likeable. But, because they work behind closed doors, they are inaccessible to the general public and therefore somewhat mysterious.

Chapter 6

Comparing the IRS and Industry — the People and the System

Key Topics

*Since my IRS experience contrasted starkly with my career in indus-
try, I cannot help but draw comparisons. In this chapter, I highlight
some of the differences and offer what I believe to be some of the
best practices in the IRS and industry.*

With the exception of a two-year period when I practiced law in New
York City, my career has been in the corporate sector in such diverse
industries as retail foods, banking, chemicals, agriculture, real estate, and
semiconductors. Since the semiconductor industry was my most recent and
longest lasting employer (22 years), I probably have the greatest appreciation for it and the high-technology sector.

Job Security

IRS employees, like many in government, are very concerned about job
security. They have told me that they do not want to be caught up in corporate downsizing, outsourcing, mergers or acquisitions.

People who choose to work in industry, especially in the high-technology
world, seem to be energized by the risk of failure, which is offset by the
thrill of potential bonuses, profit-sharing payouts, and sizeable stock
option gains. They believe that their own hard work will make their company financially strong and competitive. Should there be a merger or
acquisition, they have no doubt that theirs will be the surviving company.

Work Day

IRS employees are punctual. They typically arrive at their offices
promptly at 7:00 or 7:30 AM and leave at 4:00 or 4:30 PM. They take
lunch from 11:30 AM to 12:30 PM. Some are on flex time, where they
may work ten-hour days for four days a week. Others work nine-hour
days with every other Friday off. There are few, if any, evening meetings
and no weekend work. Employees report their time to a timekeeper.

Corporate workers tend to have more flexible hours. They do not report
their time to a timekeeper. They may come to the office later, but compen-
sate for this at the end of the day. Evening business appointments and

weekend commitments are not unusual. They are not paid for a set work schedule; they are paid for results.

Tenure

IRS employees tend to stay with the government for a long time. Employees with 15, 20, 25, 30, 35, and even 40 years of service are not uncommon. One reason for this long tenure is the nature of the government retirement system, which rewards people who stay on the job.

Corporate workers tend to move around more, especially in the early years of their careers. As they advance, they may stay longer at a single company, but retirement benefits in private industry typically are not as attractive as the government.

Employee Safety

Both the IRS and private industry care strongly about employee safety, whether it is in the nature of escaping from a burning building, maintaining clutter-free office surroundings, providing ergonomically-correct office chairs, or preventing attacks from outsiders.

I would give the safety edge to the IRS in one area — security from external attacks. Since the bombing of the federal building in Oklahoma City in 1995, the IRS enhanced its security in and around its buildings. IRS walk-in centers have security guards. All IRS office doors require special security passes. Employees continually are advised not to wear their IRS identification badges outside the building as they are probably more subject to attack than the average federal or private industry employee.

In spite of this increased level of security for IRS employees, attacks still happen. Unfortunately, this is inevitable for an agency that collects taxes from the public.

Financial Goals

IRS employees seem to be more concerned about quality-of-life issues than the achievement of lofty financial goals through long hours of work. I noticed fewer workaholics in the IRS than in industry.

Corporate workers are more willing to sacrifice personal time in order to chase the golden ring of profit sharing and stock appreciation.

Views on Business

IRS employees, usually having little real-life business background, tend to be suspicious of people in business, and historically the IRS management has done little to lessen these suspicions. I attempted to change this attitude, but with mixed results. It is hard to change long-held ingrained beliefs. Yes, there are some bad apples in the business world, but, for the most part, business people I know are honorable and want to do the right thing.

People in industry love the concept of simply being in business. They want the freedom to run a company without intrusion from government, unions, and other forces. They want the free market to rule. Government regulators, legislators, and unions are perceived as hindrances to the smooth operation of their companies.

Unions

In recent years union activity has increased in the government sectors. I am told that some 50% of eligible non-managerial IRS employees belong to the National Treasury Employees Union (NTEU). The NTEU is very powerful, influencing work hours, work assignments, salary grades, sick leave, and working environment. Generally one or two NTEU representatives join management discussions for all but the most sensitive management issues.

However, unions can slow the pace of government. For example, whenever IRS management wants to introduce a new taxpayer program, such as an initiative to reduce taxpayer compliance burden, it must get a sign-off from NTEU that this initiative is acceptable. This process can be time-consuming.

The trend in industry has been to operate without union involvement. Today only about one job in eight is represented by the unions, down significantly over the past 25 years.

Unions are virtually non-existent in the high-technology industry. Unionization efforts in this sector have failed primarily because unions could not prove to workers how membership would improve their compensation, benefits, and working conditions.

Without the obligation of dealing with unions, high-technology companies are able to respond more quickly to changes in the marketplace.

Entrepreneurship

The IRS is a bureaucratic organization. It operates from top to bottom. The top person gives orders to his subordinate, who gives orders to his subordinate, and so on. It is often considered inappropriate, unless permission is given, to jump over your boss and pass on information to someone higher up.

In this environment, creativity can sometimes be stifled. There may be no incentive to think big picture — just think within your job description. Small wage increases add little incentive to excel. Risk-taking is frowned upon. Entrepreneurship is not encouraged.

In industry, on the other hand, particularly in the high-technology world, entrepreneurship is encouraged and fostered. Many of the advances in computers, software, and biotech were inspired by the promise of good wage increases, profit-sharing, stock option grants, and the willingness to go out on a limb and take a chance.

Employee Autonomy

Some IRS employees have told me they like their jobs because there is little oversight over their work product. They are permitted a great amount of autonomy in their examination of the taxpayer, and there is hardly any higher level review. In the IRS culture, management wants to be seen supporting its troops.

I believe that this lack of work product oversight by IRS management has sometimes damaged the audit relationship between the IRS and the taxpayer.

I witnessed cases where the examiner came up with proposals that to me seemed far fetched. Even his colleagues in the office thought so, but his supervisors chose not to second guess him. The taxpayer would ask for my help as senior industry advisor. I would arrange a hearing with the top executives in my sector. More often than not, they also would be reluctant to go against the examiner's findings. This left the taxpayer with no other recourse than to move the case to the IRS Appellate Division. At this level Appeals would often concede the issue or make a major concession in favor of the taxpayer.

If this examiner's supervisors had exercised better control over the quality of his work product, taxpayer relations would have remained intact and the time of the Appeals organization would not have been wasted.

In industry, I have noticed there is better oversight of the work product as it goes through the chain. The goal is to produce an end product that will please the customer. If the product is defective, fails to meet performance criteria, is unpleasing to the eye, or is too expensive, the customer will be unhappy. As a result, there are various oversight panels to challenge the product managers at every step to make sure the product meets all of the quality specifications.

Budgets

The budget year for government agencies is October 1 to September 30. By law, agencies may not exceed their budgets, but they generally spend the entire amount. If, toward the end of the financial year, the IRS notices that budgeted funds have not been used, it will make a conscious effort to do so. Budgeted funds seldom go unused because the next year's budget will be based on the prior year's spending.

In industry, the budget constraints are different. Companies prepare a budget, and they try to adhere to it. If they sometimes exceed the budget for good reasons, they will not have broken the law. The next year's budget is based not on last year's budget or spending but rather on a projection of actual needs.

Employee Travel

It appeared to me that mid- and upper-level IRS employees traveled more than my industry colleagues. I believe some of the IRS travel is unnecessary.

I observed, for example, an area of IRS travel abuse in the Small Business/ Self-Employed Division. Many times auditors would travel across the country to audit a small business when a locally-based auditor could have performed the same function, saving the expense of air fare, hotel, car rental and meals.

I know of one egregious case where an auditor flew from Ohio to California for a small business audit, proposed a fifty dollar assessment, and returned to Ohio. This was an unfortunate waste of the IRS budget and taxpayers' money. One can imagine that reports of similar situations would make the Congress wary of IRS budget increase requests.

Hiring in Good and Bad Times

During the period 2001–2004, the Large and Mid-Size Business Division (LMSB) was authorized to hire new staff to replace retirees. This came during a period when the economy was in a recession for much of the time.

During the same period, industry reacted to the recession by downsizing its workforce. Many companies in the high-technology sector downsized by 10–40%.

Some industry executives expressed concern to me that government was adding workforce at a time when industry was going through painful reductions. I did not have a good answer for them. While the IRS was undergoing some belt-tightening, its response was not as extreme as the private sector.

Matching Staffing with the Workload

The LMSB has too many employees in some areas of the country, but they are understaffed in other areas. Union workforce rules and high living costs contribute to this problem.

When a large company leaves one city to relocate to another city, the LMSB team may find itself overstaffed. Because of union workforce rules, however, the Service may have difficulty downsizing its staff relative to the current workload requirements.

On the other hand, staffing in an area may be too lean because of high living costs, making it difficult to recruit agents. As a result, agents are overburdened with work, and audit coverage and quality may suffer.

In industry, management is given more freedom to match staff levels with customer needs, which results in cost savings and greater efficiency.

Areas of Overstaffing

There is one area in the Treasury Department/IRS that I believe is greatly overstaffed. This is in the newly created department called Treasury Inspector General for Tax Administration (TIGTA). TIGTA was created by the IRS Restructuring and Reform Act of 1998 to audit IRS employees. With a staff of 1000, there is one TIGTA employee for every 100 IRS employees.

In contrast to this, industry employs about one or two internal auditors for every 1000 employees. TIGTA has five to ten times as many auditors per employees as private industry.

Some IRS employees find TIGTA to be intrusive and obstructive, going so far as to claim that it is the U.S. government's counterpart to the Russian KGB. In many IRS circles it is feared. TIGTA seems to be everywhere, perhaps because its auditors have enough time on their hands to make unnecessary requests for reports and investigations.

In my view the TIGTA staff could easily be reduced by one-half. This would free up cash resources that could be used by the Service for other programs, such as hiring auditors to audit tax shelters and other suspicious returns.

I believe Congress should commence a review of the TIGTA organization, using private industry benchmarks, to determine a more appropriate auditor/employee ratio.

Getting the Product to Market

I use the term "products" in a very broad sense in the context of LMSB. We could be talking about the very long time it takes to conduct a corporate audit. Or we could be talking about the delayed introduction of electronic tax returns for corporations, originally scheduled for 2002 and finally put in place in 2005.

The IRS has been notoriously late at getting many of its products to market. One example of this is the sluggish release of regulations, rulings, and other types of advice coming from the Chief Counsel's Office. These "products" are the various forms of guidance that are so critical to the efficiency of the LMSB organization in its dealings with its taxpayer base.

What makes this process so slow? Is the Service trying to get too many products out to the public at one time? Is the review process too complex? For whatever reason, the Service cannot seem to meet its deadlines.

I will attempt to compare its IRS guidance process with the way the computer industry views the production and distribution schedule when it is planning to introduce a new product.

If we are talking about a new computer model that we want to have on the market just before school begins, we know that it has to be on the store shelves in late July or early August. There can be no delays. If the computers arrive in January of the next year, we are late to market and our business may not survive. Our company CEO must be vigilant in insisting that the computers go through the R & D, manufacturing and sales process to arrive on the shelves in late July or early August. There are no excuses.

In government, however, the issue of accountability may be the problem. The IRS counterpart to the company CEO is the Secretary of the Treasury. He has jurisdiction over all of the key players: the Chief Counsel's Office, the Assistant Secretary of the Treasury for Tax Policy, the Commissioner of the Internal Revenue Service, and the Commissioner of the LMSB.

He is responsible for making sure that the guidance (the product) reaches taxpayers in a timely manner. He should insist that the departments communicate with each other and work as a team to make this happen.

Sadly, I am told the Secretary of the Treasury hardly interacts with most of these other offices. Yes, they talk to each other, but there is no one holding their feet to the fire. Additionally, the tenure of the Secretary of the Treasury is often of short duration, thus making it difficult for the individual to gain a full understanding of the complexities of the post.

The System: Getting from A to B

In industry, especially in the high technology world I came from, it seemed relatively easy to get from A to B. You would set a goal and move straight ahead to achieve it. Of course there would be obstacles, such as the need to invent the product, obtain the right manufacturing capability, and attract the right customer base to purchase your product. The challenges can be huge, but your efforts will not be hindered by bureaucracy.

In my experience with the IRS, which I believe is typical of many government agencies, it is not as easy to go directly from A to B. Senior managers from industry who join government have a common lament. They wanted to make a difference but discovered that the constraints of bureaucracy will not let them do so.

In LMSB we often heard complaints about the length of time corporate audits were taking. We wanted to shorten the process. This seemed simple enough. But to move forward meant getting the unions involved, and then counsel, Treasury and the operating groups, and beyond that, we thought it would be wise to seek comments from various external organizations. Before we knew it, the process had become mired in bureaucratic red tape to such an extent that nothing meaningful was accomplished.

If an outsider unfamiliar with IRS bureaucracy had tried to lead this effort, he or she would have been overwhelmed with complexity and protocol.

I very much admired the government employees, usually the more experienced personnel, who had learned to navigate the system. To get from A to B, they would go to D, then to J, then to R, back to K, then to W, but end up at B. These people are invaluable to the efforts of the IRS.

Part Two:
The World of the Large and Mid-Size Business Division

Chapter 7

IRS Initiatives

Key Topics

Since the establishment of the Large and Mid-Size Business Division (LMSB), many taxpayer-friendly compliance initiatives have been initiated. The following are the most important of these initiatives:

1. Pre-Filing Agreements (PFAs)

2. Industry Issue Resolution Agreements (IIRs)

3. Limited Issue Focused Examinations (LIFE)

4. Fast Track Appeals

5. Tax Shelter Settlement Initiatives

6. Joint Audit Planning Process

7. Schedule M-3 to the Form 1120

8. Compliance Assurance Process (CAP)

9. Corporate e-file

These initiatives are in addition to other taxpayer compliance initiatives in existence prior to the formation of LMSB:

1. Accelerated Issue Resolution (AIR) Agreements

2. Delegation Order 236

3. Delegation Order 4-25 (formerly Delegation Order 247)

4. Early Referral to Appeals

These earlier initiatives provided a good start in streamlining the audit process:

1. Accelerated Issue Resolution (AIR) Agreements: Allows the Team Manager to extend resolution of the same or similar issues from one tax period to later tax periods.

2. Delegation Order 236: Gives the LMSB Team Manager the authority to settle an issue with the taxpayer where Appeals has previously settled the same issue of the taxpayer in an earlier audit or where Appeals has settled the issue of another taxpayer directly involved in the transaction or taxable event. The facts must remain the same as in

the settled period, and the legal authority on the issue must be unchanged.

3. Delegation Order 4-25: Gives the LMSB Team Manager the authority to settle an issue with the taxpayer based on written settlement guidelines from Appeals.

4. Early Referral to Appeals: Permits the taxpayer to request that a developed unagreed issue in an on-going examination may be referred to Appeals prior to the conclusion of the examination. Early referral may only be made where the remaining issues under examination are not expected to be completed before Appeals could resolve the early referral issue.

Pre-Filing Agreements (PFAs)

The first LMSB initiative was a program designed to resolve complex factual issues prior to filing of the tax return. Under the Pre-Filing Agreement (PFA) program the taxpayer and the IRS collectively would try to resolve a set of factual issues by applying well-settled principles of law to the facts. Initially limited to the filing date plus extensions, the program was later expanded to allow a resolution to extend to up to four years beyond the current year.

The PFA program reduces taxpayer burden and makes more effective use of IRS resources by eliminating tax controversy before the tax return is filed and providing certainty that agreed upon tax positions will not be challenged during the post-filing examination process.

The PFA program has been useful in resolving factual issues in a number of areas, including the Research & Experimental Tax Credit, mergers and acquisitions, and valuations of property.

Industry Issue Resolution Agreements (IIRs)

Certain business tax issues are frequently disputed or burdensome to a significant number of taxpayers. Industry Issue Resolution Agreements (IIRs) provide some guidance in resolving these issues.

IIR issues should have at least two of the following characteristics:

1. Proper tax treatment of a common factual situation is uncertain.

2. Uncertainty results in frequent, often repetitive examinations of the same issue.

3. Uncertainty results in taxpayer burden.

4. The issue is significant and impacts a large number of taxpayers either within an industry or across industry lines.

5. The issue requires extensive factual development, and an understanding of industry practices and views concerning the issue would assist in determining the proper tax treatment.

The IIR process is not appropriate to an individual or a small number of taxpayers, to transactions lacking a *bona fide* business purpose, to transactions with a significant purpose of improperly reducing or avoiding federal taxes, or to transfer pricing matters or international treaties.

From the IIR process will usually come guidance in the form of a revenue procedure or revenue ruling. It may also include other forms of administrative guidance. It is generally applicable to future years.

Numerous IIRs have been issued in such diverse areas as the tax treatment for small wares for restaurants and taverns, demonstrator autos and dealership employees, bad debt issues for banks, golf course greens, abandoned movie and TV scripts for the entertainment industry, and railroad tracks.

Limited Issue Focused Examinations (LIFE)

An alternative to the traditional, full-scope examination process, the Limited Issue Focused Examination (LIFE) process is a streamlined, issue-focused plan for examining those issues representing the greatest compliance risk. The goal is to provide a quality examination with the least burden to both the taxpayer and the government.

The most critical factor in a LIFE examination is the application of materiality principles to limit scope. LIFE focuses on those issues most consequential to the overall tax liability, thereby addressing the greatest compliance risks.

LIFE requires LMSB to enter into a Memorandum of Understanding (MOU) with a taxpayer to govern key aspects of the examination. The MOU identifies the issues to be examined and the materiality thresholds to govern any expansion in the scope of the examination. The MOU requires cooperation between the examiner and the taxpayer to complete the examination. If the taxpayer does not meet the commitments in the MOU, the process may be terminated. The scope of the examination may then be expanded to include some or all of the large, unusual and/or questionable items identified in the risk analysis.

Tax Shelter Settlement Initiatives

The IRS has devoted a significant percentage of its staff resources to combat abusive tax shelters. Many of these shelters have been listed in a Revenue Ruling as "listed transactions."

There are thousands of abusive tax shelter transactions. In order to save itself time and resources, the IRS has proposed a variety of settlement initiatives for many of these shelters. Generally the taxpayer must agree to pay most or all of the tax he or she attempted to avoid, plus interest. Penalties that may be applicable include negligence, accuracy and civil and criminal fraud. In some of the settlement initiatives, some or all of these penalties have been waived.

Fast Track Appeals

Fast Track Appeals is a program designed to bring the taxpayer, the IRS examiner, and an Appeals officer together during the examination process of the return to try to settle one or a few contested issues. The program eliminates the need for the taxpayer to formally go to Appeals. While in Fast Track, LMSB keeps jurisdiction of the case. In this program, the issues must be significantly developed as to facts and law, and there must be a good-efforts attempt among the parties to reach settlement. Assuming settlement is not reached, the taxpayer still has the right to take the issue to Appeals.

The benefit of this procedure is that it is fast, efficient, and cost-effective for both the taxpayer and the government. Most of the cases in the Fast Track Appeals Settlement program close within 60–90 days. This represents a huge savings of time; normally an Appeals case could take 500–600 days.

Joint Audit Planning Process

The joint audit planning process was initiated by LMSB and the Tax Executives Institute to speed up the audit process.

Once an LMSB taxpayer has been selected for examination, the objective of the joint planning process is to bring together the key IRS audit participants and the key taxpayer participants before the audit begins.

The key participants from the IRS side might be the team manager, the team coordinator, and various specialists, including computer audit specialists, international examiners, financial products examiners, engineers, economists, employment tax examiners, excise tax examiners, and tax exempt plan examiners.

From the taxpayer's side might be specialists in asset depreciation, computer systems, the research credit, international transactions, tax exempt plans, and deferred compensation plans.

Critical to the success of the process is communication, trust, and openness. Both the taxpayer and the IRS should share a common goal of completing the examination in the most efficient manner.

At the start of the examination and prior to the opening conference, the taxpayer and the Service should meet and exchange information essential to the preparation of a quality risk analysis of the items on the return that may have a material tax impact. The goal is to reduce the items examined on the return to the ones that are most important from the standpoint of potential tax collection.

The IRS and taxpayer should candidly discuss potential issues and required compliance checks early in the planning phase so that the taxpayer can make the necessary resources available when needed. The taxpayer can help reduce examination time by providing a meaningful company orientation to the audit team.

After successfully completing the initial steps of the joint audit planning process, including agreement as to the allocation of resources and at what times, the IRS will furnish a draft audit plan to the taxpayer for review and concurrence. If the taxpayer concurs, the audit is then ready to begin.

IRS managers and agents tell me they like the joint audit planning process and think it has done much to speed up the audit.

Schedule M-3 to the Form 1120

The purpose of the Schedule M-3 is to make differences between financial accounting net income and taxable income on the Form 1120 easier for the IRS to spot and understand.

Schedule M-3 provides information that identifies taxpayers who may have engaged in aggressive transactions and therefore should be audited. The disclosures requested in the Schedule M-3 help target high-risk areas, thereby improving and speeding up the audit process. At the same time, the Schedule M-3 will serve as a screening process to eliminate the audits of taxpayers who have not engaged in aggressive transactions.

Compliance Assurance Process (CAP) Program

The Compliance Assurance Process (CAP) is a new approach to the auditing of publicly traded corporations. Through CAP, the IRS will work with taxpayers during the filing year using a variety of third party information sources (*e.g.*, filings with the Securities and Exchange Commission) to identify and resolve issues of controversy in real time. Taxpayers and IRS representatives will sign an MOU to ensure commitment on issues such as cooperation, transparency, and timely access to records and personnel.

CAP will be made available to LMSB taxpayers who have had a history of honest dealings and have established trust and rapport with the IRS. Taxpayers having contentious audit histories with the IRS may not be offered CAP.

Issues that cannot be resolved through the CAP process will move to the more traditional post-filing process. It is likely that many CAP audits will have a few unresolved issues remaining that may need to go to Appeals or the courts.

CAP should help the Service shorten the time it takes to audit corporate returns, with fewer staff resources, improve overall compliance results, and help identify abusive tax shelter transactions more quickly.

I predict that CAP will become the favored filing process by large companies. Quality taxpayers will want to tell others in their industry that they are viewed as good taxpayers by using the CAP process. Company CEOs will want their companies in the CAP program because it, like the Malcolm Baldridge Quality Award, will signify a quality company known for its honesty and fair dealing.

Corporate E-File

Corporate e-file is an extension of the electronic filing process that is currently available to individual taxpayers. It will permit LMSB taxpayers to file their Forms 1120 and 1120S and accompanying schedules electronically.

For tax year 2005 returns due in 2006, IRS regulations require that corporations with total assets of $50 million or more file their Forms 1120 and 1120S electronically.

Beginning in 2007, the electronic filing requirement will be expanded to include the tax year 2006 tax returns of corporations with $10 million or more in total assets.

The electronic filing requirements only apply to entities that file at least 250 returns during a calendar year, including income tax, excise tax, information, and employment tax returns.

The Service believes that electronic filing will help speed tax processing and reduce audit cycle time. Taxpayers will benefit from electronic filing by resolving uncertainties earlier, thus saving interest expense. This is important because audits for large corporations take an average of five years to complete.

Speedier processing will also help the IRS identify emerging trends and abuses, thereby enabling the Service to address problems such as abusive tax avoidance transactions before they get out of hand.

Chapter 8

IRS Audit Concerns

Key Topics

During my four-year term as Senior Industry Advisor for the Communications, Technology and Media Group, I was privileged to sit with the senior leadership team of the Large and Mid-Size Business Division (LMSB) and discuss issues of importance now and into the future. LMSB has many challenges: shortening the audit time for corporations, increasing the number of corporations that are audited, replacing agents who have retired, dealing with ever more complex tax laws, and coping with abusive tax shelters.

Length of Audit Time

One of the major challenges for the LMSB organization is the length of time it takes to conduct a corporate audit.

It is not unusual for the audit of a company to take up to 60 months or more. This does not include the time it takes to appeal the case or go to the courts. I know of instances where corporate audits have lasted 120–180 months.

Lengthy audits have proven to be disadvantageous to both the taxpayer and the Service. Taxpayers may find that they are unable to retrieve records from earlier periods of time, particularly if there have been staff changes and the current company tax personnel were not on staff when the initial tax calculations were made. In addition, they are incurring interest expense during the audit period. The Service also suffers because it has difficulty understanding the tax calculations and records after such a long period of time has lapsed.

LMSB is attempting to speed up the audit process from several directions.

1. Get high audit risk returns to agents faster. Historically it has taken about 18 months to get returns from the IRS Service Centers. All of this work has now been consolidated in the Ogden, Utah Service Center. Through various efficiency measures, the Service is hopeful that this time can be cut in half.

2. Encourage taxpayers to respond more quickly to information requests. Slow Information Document Request (IDR) response times significantly hinder audit conclusions. I have witnessed some

improvement here. Interestingly, IDR response times seem to be faster with the new line companies (most of which are on the West Coast) than the old line companies of the Mid-West and East Coast.

3. Take advantage of IRS initiatives such as Pre-Filing Agreements, Industry Issue Resolution Agreements, Limited Issue Focused Examinations (LIFE), Fast Track Appeals, Corporate e-file, the Joint Audit Planning Process, and the Compliance Assurance Process (CAP) program. These initiatives are explained in Chapter Seven. Unfortunately, many taxpayers and auditors are unfamiliar or uncomfortable with these initiatives, and many of them have not yet been widely used.

4. Expedite older case closings. The IRS used expedited case closing procedures in 2003 and 2004 as a way to close out older cases. Auditors were directed to focus on the critical and most material issues of their cases and to close them by a date certain. These procedures proved effective in closing out a significant number of open taxable years for companies and reducing the audit time for statistical purposes.

5. Use other older, but perhaps forgotten initiatives, such as Accelerated Issue Resolution (AIR) Agreements and Delegation Orders 236 and 4-25 (formerly Delegation Order 247). See Chapter Seven for a review of these initiatives.

6. Use the Industry Director's Directive with more frequency. This directive is a form of guidance where the Industry Director can limit certain types of audits because of Service manpower resource limitations. For example, this directive has been applied or is being considered in the areas of cost segregation of assets in the construction of buildings and in capitalization versus expensing of transaction costs in mergers and acquisitions where the taxpayer presents positions on its return that are within ranges acceptable to the Service based on prior audit resolution history at the examination and appeals levels.

Inadequate LMSB Coverage of All Taxpayers

LMSB audits only a fraction of the corporations defined as large and mid-sized businesses. The remainder are seldom audited and, as a result, have become generally more aggressive in their behavior.

The goal of LMSB is to audit corporations more quickly in order to free up staff resources to audit more corporations. The new Compliance Assurance Process (CAP) program and the Schedule M-3 to the Form 1120 (see Chapter Seven for more information on CAP and the Schedule M-3) should permit LMSB to screen companies faster and go on to others that should be audited.

The Aging of the LMSB Workforce

LMSB is working hard to meet the challenge of maintaining a quality workforce in the face of many retirements. In the ten-year period from LMSB's establishment, as many as 50–75% of its workforce will retire.

An aggressive hiring campaign, both internally and externally, is under way. It will be a challenge to bring in people who can fill the knowledge gap. People leaving often have up to 25–40 years of quality experience while their replacements are individuals with only 5–10 years of quality experience. The knowledge gap of 20–30 years may be an insurmountable obstacle.

Some of the replacements are coming from the Small Business/Self-Employed Division, but most new hires are coming from accounting firms and corporate tax departments.

The Complexity of the Tax Law

The Service must constantly confront the challenge of administering new and more complex tax laws. My personal experience is that as tax laws become more complex, tax planning for the corporate sector tends to become more creative. IRS employees who have just come up to speed with the old laws will now have to comprehend and detect new tax-planning strategies, some of which will be legal and some of which will be questionable.

Inadequate Distribution of Staff Resources

The IRS has an imbalance of revenue agents relative to companies in their geographic territories. This is particularly true where one or more companies have left an IRS geographic region and moved to another region half way across the country. Other parts of the country may have too few agents. This is true in high cost-of-living areas such as San Francisco and New York City.

Inadequate Training

While agents appear to be well trained in the corporate tax laws, they have sometimes proved to be deficient in the areas of partnership and trust taxation. These deficiencies put them at a disadvantage when they audit taxpayers with abusive tax shelter transactions structured as complex partnerships and trusts.

Cases Moving to Appeals

Many agents in LMSB find it challenging to prepare their cases in a sufficiently tight manner as to avoid reversals in whole or part at the Appeals stage. It is disheartening for them to prepare their cases for audit, set up proposed additional tax assessments, and send the cases to Appeals, only to have their cases compromised by an Appeals Officer.

Abusive Tax Shelters

LMSB is confronting head-on the proliferation of new abusive tax shelters. Such work is very time-consuming. About one-fifth of LMSB's resources currently are devoted to such shelters. LMSB hopes to eradicate this problem so that it can turn its resources to normal corporate audits. It will be in the best interests of everyone if these cases can be disposed of through quicker procedures. Presently they are just accumulating with no apparent resolution in sight. I believe the Service should begin to aggressively use settlement initiatives to reduce the caseload build-up.

Chapter 9

HINTS TO CONDUCTING A SUCCESSFUL AUDIT

Key Topics

In the four years that I spent with the Large and Mid-Size Business Division (LMSB), I believe I picked up many helpful hints about conducting an audit. These hints should be useful to corporate tax professionals and their representatives from the legal and accounting professions.

Let me start by saying that when I was in the private sector, I did not spend much time directly dealing with IRS auditors. I was more involved with tax research and strategic planning. My staff and I worked energetically to substantiate various tax positions taken. This was especially true in the transfer pricing area of products and services, operations of overseas controlled subsidiaries, the Research and Experimental Tax Credit, and the depreciation of capital assets.

The compliance function at Advanced Micro Devices reported to me, and it was through this reporting relationship that I had dealings with the IRS. This involvement generally occurred when there were problems that had to be resolved during or at the conclusion of the audit.

Nonetheless, I endeavored to be a major influence on the audit. I set the audit tone with my compliance staff. I wanted them to treat the auditors fairly and honestly and to be responsive to their requests. It was important to me that my staff and I had a relationship of trust and rapport with the IRS auditors.

Now, having seen audit issues from the perspective of the private sector and the IRS, I offer the following observations of worthwhile audit practices in the spirit of good tax administration.

Develop Trust and Rapport with the IRS Team

This can begin even before you start an audit. If you have the opportunity to meet some of the IRS team in non-audit settings, such as at joint industry/IRS Tax Executives Institute programs, or at American Institute of Certified Public Accountants or American Bar Association programs, this connection will go a long way to starting the relationship. Serving on a tax panel with them can also be useful in beginning to understand issues from their perspective.

Once you are in the audit relationship, it is important to reach out to the auditors. You can begin to build trust and gain rapport by encouraging your team to have joint coffee breaks with the IRS team. In general, it is essential to follow through on your commitments with the IRS team to show your willingness to cooperate.

If you have not had very much experience conducting an audit, I recommend that you start the process by consulting with an IRS expert in one of the accounting or law firms. Some of these consultants may have recently worked for the IRS and could have top-level IRS contacts and experience. These individuals can help you set the right tone for your audit and assist with audit strategy and relationship-building in a manner that will ensure the quickest and most satisfying resolution.

Work with the IRS Team on Information Document Requests (IDRs)

Sit down with the IRS team prior to the drafting of every IDR and discuss the purpose of the document and what the Service hopes to achieve from it. Once the IDR is drafted, review it again to see if it is germane to the issue the Service is examining. You and the IRS team may need to re-draft the IDR to narrow its scope. I prefer that an IDR be issued for every single issue. Multiple issue IDRs can be cumbersome, and responses to them can sometimes be confusing.

Live Up to IDR Response Times

Try to be as punctual as you can. Ideally you will respond to each IDR in about ten days for domestic IDRs and 20 days for international IDRs. Some companies respond to IDR requests much more quickly, handling domestic requests in about three days and international requests in about five days. It is appropriate that you reach an agreement with the IRS team to provide feedback to your IDR responses on a timely basis.

Try to set the ground rules with the IRS team so that IDR requests are spaced out. It is difficult to respond to large numbers of requests when they arrive at the same time.

If you are having trouble meeting an IDR deadline, let the IRS team know as soon as possible. Sometimes the information you need is difficult to retrieve. At other times, you may not have the staff available to respond because of sickness, layoffs, or other audit work coming in at the same time (*e.g.*, state income tax, sales and use tax, and property tax audits). The IRS audit team will appreciate this advance notice as it will help them schedule their team members to work on other projects.

Be a Straight Shooter

When auditors ask a question, give them your best answer. If you do not know, tell them so and offer to find the answer. Sometimes an intuitive response can also be helpful, especially when it is followed up by good documentation.

Don't Play Games

Don't tell the auditors you will obtain information for them, and then at the last minute tell them the information does not exist. Don't try to lead them into wild goose chases by implying that a certain transaction may have additional potential tax audit liability when it does not.

Try to be as responsive to the IRS request as you can. If the IRS team asks for information about a foreign subsidiary, don't give the team 100 boxes of information when a two-page response would be more appropriate.

Maintain Your Credibility

I believe that your word is your bond. Once you demonstrate that your actions support your words, the IRS team will be more likely to trust you in the future. If you tell them that an area under review probably does not have tax issues worth pursuing, they may go along with your suggestion. But, if they later learn through some other source that they have been mis-led, you may have destroyed your entire relationship of goodwill.

Use the IRS Initiatives

If possible, use initiatives such as the Joint Audit Planning Process, Pre-Filing Agreements, Industry Issue Resolutions, Limited Issue Focused Examinations (LIFE), Fast Track Appeals, Early Referral to Appeals, Accelerated Issue Resolutions (AIR) Agreements, and Delegation Orders 236 and 4-25 (formerly Delegation Order 247). See Chapter Seven for a discussion of these initiatives.

Participate in Industry and Professional Meetings

Engage the IRS in tax administration discussions. Aside from meetings with members of the Tax Executives Institute, the American Institute of Certified Public Accountants, and the American Bar Association, there may be other occasions where you can join a smaller industry-specific group to discuss issues with the IRS leadership in your industry.

I participated in many industry-specific meetings as Senior Industry Advisor for the Communications, Technology and Media Group. My Industry Director and the Directors of Field Operations looked forward to meeting with specific industry groups in the areas of telecommunications and wireless, cable, high-technology hardware and software, the movie industry, publishing, music recording, gaming and sports.

From these meetings the top IRS leadership learned about problems faced by more than one company and often would take action to lessen the problems for the industry sector. These top leaders also encouraged the industry executives to contact them if they had a problem with their audit or if they felt that their audit and others in the industry could be handled in a better way.

Don't Hesitate to Ask for a Summons

The case may arise where you may need the help of a "friendly summons."

For example, you may not be able to legally give third party information to the IRS without the cover of a summons. This could happen if you have information about another company with which you have a business relationship.

Or you may need a summons to convince your boss (perhaps the chief financial officer) that you need additional staff to comply with the information requested in the summons. A summons will show the boss the seriousness of your problem.

Dispose of Disputed Tax Items as You Go Along in the Audit

Some tax professionals like to hold all of their disputed items to the end of the audit and then try to negotiate the best possible deal for their company, taking into account all of these disputed audit issues.

However, by disposing of issues as you work through the audit, you will be able to complete the overall audit more quickly, saving staff time and interest expense. And, in so doing, you will also foster a better working relationship with the IRS team.

Set Aggressive Time Lines for Completion of the Audit

The IRS is under pressure to complete audits more quickly and to have fewer years of unaudited returns open at any one time. They want to complete the audit as soon as possible.

As a taxpayer, you will benefit by reducing your interest cost on audit adjustments, and you will be able to eliminate tax audit reserves in your financial statements at an earlier time. This should please your shareholders.

Be Professional

Don't take the audit personally. Remember that your job is to represent your company's financial interests and pay no more taxes than you legally owe. The IRS audit team's job is to represent the U.S. government and collect the appropriate amount of taxes owed by your company.

You may have areas of disagreement about the exact amount that is owed. It is okay to disagree. This disagreement may cause you to take an issue to IRS Appeals, and subsequently to U.S. Tax Court or a federal district court. Nevertheless, you should not let this disagreement destroy the overall IRS audit relationship.

Chapter 10

CONGRESS AND THE IRS

Key Topics

The U.S. Congress has a considerable impact on the IRS.

The Congress passes tax laws that the IRS must help interpret and administer. The Congress controls the budget of the IRS. The Congress has oversight authority over the IRS. The Congress, through the Joint Tax Committee, monitors large requests for tax refunds.

Law Changes

Every year Congress passes new tax laws. In some years the IRS is required to administer a large number of changes in a very short time frame. The tax law changes are usually finalized in the latter part of a year at a signing of the tax bill by the president. The IRS must then mobilize its best talent to prepare tax return forms, instructions, questions and answers and other guidance to help taxpayers comply with the new law changes.

The American Jobs Creation Act of 2004 illustrates the nimbleness required of the IRS.

It took considerable effort on the part of the two tax writing committees of the Congress, the Ways and Means Committee of the House of Representatives and the Senate Finance Committee of the U.S. Senate, to pass this legislation.

Bill Thomas, the Chairman of the Ways and Means Committee, did an admirable job of bringing together into one bill the differing views of the 24 Republican members and 17 Democratic members of the committee while Charles Grassley, the Chairman of the Senate Finance Committee, expended a similar effort in producing a bill that incorporated the views of the 11 Republicans and 9 Democrats of his committee.

The two bills were then reviewed and debated by a smaller House-Senate Tax Conference Committee. The final product was the American Jobs Creation Act of 2004.

Upon passage of the Act, the IRS responded with great efficiency. New tax forms, with instructions, were drafted. All areas of the IRS were involved in the process.

The Large and Mid-Size Business Division (LMSB) began to mobilize even before the Act became final. Its tax policy experts looked at both the House and Senate versions and planned what-if scenarios. Some parts of the new tax law would apply retroactively to 2004 and required immediate guidance as to how certain types of transactions should be handled for corporate taxpayers.

LMSB, in coordination with LMSB Division Counsel and the IRS Chief Counsel's Office, used considerable resources to review scenarios covered by the law as well as those not covered directly by the law but which also needed answers. No fewer than 500 people from LMSB and many people from Treasury were involved in the smooth interpretation of the new law.

IRS Budget

The IRS depends for its budget on the House and Senate Appropriations Committees. The House Appropriations Committee has over 60 members and the Senate Appropriations Committee has about 30 members.

These two committees approve the various federal government agency budgets. The IRS comes within the Treasury budget, which has recently been in the range of 11–12 billion dollars. The overwhelming portion of the Treasury budget goes to the IRS budget, which is in the range of 10–11 billion dollars.

The balance of the Treasury budget goes to such departments as the offices of the Comptroller of the Currency, Thrift Supervision, United States Mint, Bureau of Engraving and Printing, Financial Crimes Enforcement Network, Alcohol Tobacco Tax and Trade Bureau, the Assistant Secretary for Tax Policy, Treasury Inspector General for Tax Administration (TIGTA) and General Counsel.

Refer to the Treasury Department organization chart in Figure 10-1 to see the other departments that receive funding.

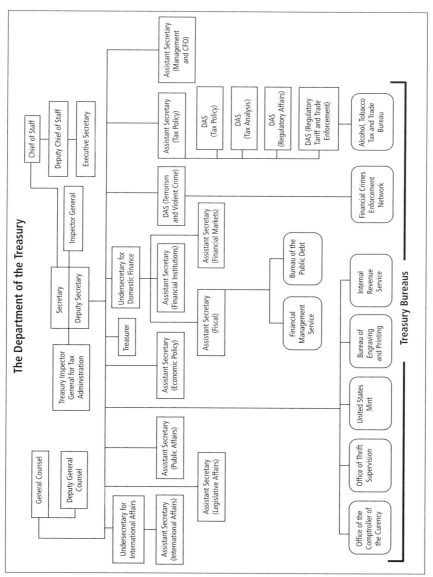

Figure 10-1: Department of the Treasury Structure.

The IRS usually asks for a larger budget than it receives, and Congress generally allows a small increase from the prior year. While this may seem positive, the IRS actually receives fewer real dollars for its programs after 3–4% wage increases are factored in for the new budget year. Since most of the costs in the budget relate to wages, the IRS has had to reduce other programs, such as travel, computer modernization, and continuing professional education of its agents.

Congressional Oversight

The IRS is often in a love-hate relationship with the Congress. While the IRS must administer the tax laws passed by Congress, it also receives criticism from Congress for the manner in which it administers the laws. Complaints of IRS wrongdoing or poor taxpayer service are heard by the Oversight Subcommittee of the Ways and Means Committee and the Taxation and IRS Oversight Subcommittee of the Senate Finance Committee.

In 1998, for example, Congress chastised the IRS for being too tough and intrusive with taxpayers. This resulted in the enactment of the IRS Restructuring and Reform Act of 1998. Several taxpayer safeguards were incorporated into this legislation. Penalties, including possible termination, were inserted in the law as consequences for breach of these safeguards by IRS staff.

With this legislation came the addition of a new Treasury Department office. Called the Office of the Treasury Inspector General for Tax Administration (TIGTA), its goal is to provide independent oversight of IRS activities. TIGTA audits are designed to promote efficiency and effectiveness in the administration of the internal revenue laws. TIGTA is dedicated to the prevention and detection of fraud, waste, and abuse in the administration of taxes. By shepherding the activities of IRS employees and programs, it makes sure that the Service is free of employee abuse and that IRS programs are adding value to the government. It does this with a staff of about 1000 employees.

Congress has its own investigatory body — the General Accounting Office (GAO) — that examines tax practices and procedures of the IRS. Recent GAO examinations of the LMSB organization have been in the areas of business systems modernization, tax shelters, international tax haven companies, and internal controls and accounting procedures. The GAO reports to the Comptroller of the Currency.

One has only to read the daily newspapers to observe that members of the House or the Senate have chastised the IRS for one problem or another and have asked for an investigation. The IRS expends considerable resources in following up on congressional requests for information. Unfortunately, many of these complaints have turned out to be unfounded.

While the IRS is often deserving of praise from the Congress, praise is seldom given; instead, members seem to feel that they will look better in the eyes of their constituents when they use the IRS as a whipping boy.

Joint Committee on Taxation

Decisions on matters such as tax refund requests from large corporations are made by the Joint Committee on Taxation, a committee composed of Republicans and Democrats from both the Ways and Means and Senate Finance Committees. These refund requests usually arise from tax years with net operating losses.

The Joint Committee on Taxation has many other important duties. By statute, these duties include reviewing the operation and effects of the federal tax laws and the administration of taxes by the IRS. Always intimately involved in tax bills, the Joint Committee analyzes the impact various tax proposals have on the cost of the bill and suggests ways to reduce the cost by modifying tax proposals or suggesting new types of activities to be taxed.

Chapter 11

IRS Counsel and the Large and Mid-Size Business Division

Key Topics

Since the establishment of the Large and Mid-Size Business Division (LMSB), IRS Counsel has had a close relationship with the LMSB organization. A new Division Counsel structure was put in place that has a dotted-line reporting relationship to LMSB. Division Counsel continues to report directly to the IRS Chief Counsel's Office.

Overview of Counsel Reporting Structure

The General Counsel of the Treasury reports to the Deputy Secretary of the Treasury, who reports to the Secretary of the Treasury (see the organization chart in Figure 11-1).

The Chief Counsel of the IRS reports to the General Counsel of the Treasury (see the organization chart in Figure 11-2).

The Division Counsel of LMSB reports to the Deputy Chief Counsel (Operations) of the IRS. The Division Counsel is co-located with the Division Commissioner of LMSB (see Figure 11-3) and has no formal reporting relationship to the LMSB Commissioner.

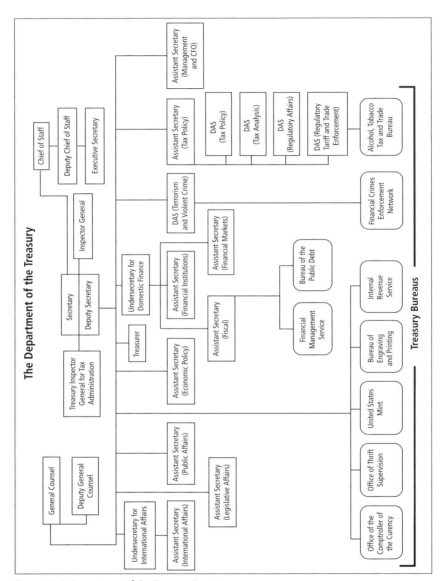

Figure 11-1: Department of the Treasury Structure.

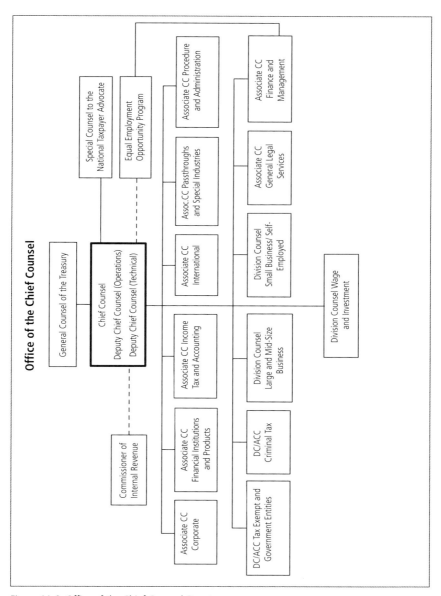

Figure 11-2: Office of the Chief Counsel Structure.

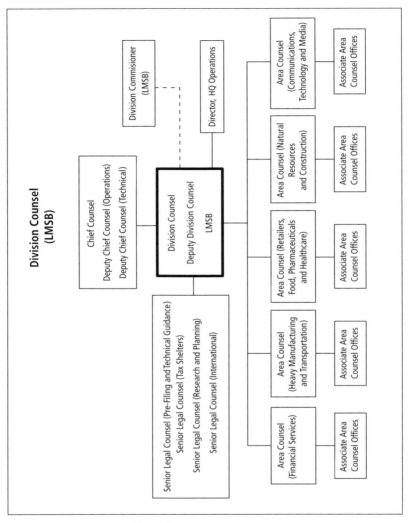

Figure 11-3: Division Counsel (LMSB).

LMSB Division Counsel

As noted in the organization chart in Figure 11-3, five Area Counsels report to the Division Counsel and are co-located with the Industry Director. The five areas are:

Area 1 — Manhattan, NY	Financial Services
Area 2 — Iselin, NJ	Heavy Manufacturing and Transportation
Area 3 — Downers Grove, IL	Retailers, Food, Pharmaceuticals and Healthcare
Area 4 — Houston, TX	Natural Resources and Construction
Area 5 — Oakland, CA	Communications, Technology and Media

Of note in all of the Counsel reporting responsibilities is that the LMSB has no direct reporting control over Counsel. Counsel views LMSB as a client, but Counsel is not under the control of LMSB for various performance measurements, such as meeting time schedules or taking positions sought by LMSB management. While Counsel and LMSB try to work in harmony, Counsel really is and can be independent of LMSB when it wants to be. LMSB does have a say in the evaluation of LMSB Counsel's services and whether they are satisfactory.

LMSB Division Counsel has almost 300 attorneys located in 36 cities around the country. These attorneys help revenue agents research complex tax issues, occasionally participating in the drafting of information document requests (IDRs), including the use of the summons power when necessary in order to obtain information. They also assist in drafting industry position papers used by agents to assure uniform auditing treatment across the country and help develop the legal research that aids in the drafting of regulations, revenue rulings and procedures, and industry director directives. Finally, they prepare for and argue cases in tax court.

Most of these attorneys are attached to an industry subgroup. They are aligned with an industry technical advisor, serving as a resource to IRS agents and management as specialists in an area. They also teach continuing professional education to agents in this field.

Attorney Subgroup Specializations in the Domestic Arena

- Aerospace
- Agriculture
- Air Transportation
- Biotech
- Capitalization
- Captive and Offshore Insurance Transactions
- Changes in Accounting Methods
- Commercial Banking and Savings and Loan
- Consolidated Corporate Returns
- Construction
- Cooperatives
- Entertainment (Movies)
- Gaming
- High Technology
- Inventory
- Leasing
- Life Insurance
- Media (Publishing)
- Mergers and Acquisitions
- Mining
- Motor Vehicles
- Partnerships
- Petroleum
- Pharmaceuticals
- Property and Casualty Insurance
- Railroads
- Research Credit
- Retail
- Security and Financial Services
- Shipping
- Sports
- Telecommunications
- Utilities

Attorney Subgroup Specializations in the International Arena

- Foreign Joint Ventures and Partnerships
- Foreign Mergers and Acquisitions
- Foreign Sales Corporations/Extraterritorial Income Exclusion
- Foreign Tax Credit
- Intercompany Pricing — Transfer Pricing
- International Penalties
- Offshore Compliance
- Permanent Establishment
- Subpart F Income

Division Counsel forms a close link with the technical branches of the Office of the Chief Counsel. They work closely with the attorneys reporting up to the Deputy Chief Counsel (Technical), who reports to the Chief Counsel.

Deputy Chief Counsel (Technical)

Several hundred attorneys report to the Deputy Chief Counsel (Technical). They include Associate Chief Counsel Corporate, Associate Chief Counsel Financial Institutions and Products, Associate Chief Counsel Income Tax and Accounting, Associate Chief Counsel International, and Associate Chief Counsel Passthroughs and Special Industries.

These attorneys have primary responsibility for drafting all published guidance within the IRS, including regulations, revenue rulings and procedures, and they work closely in this guidance process with the Office of the Assistant Secretary of the Treasury for Tax Policy.

Chapter 12

IRS APPEALS AND THE LARGE AND MID-SIZE BUSINESS DIVISION

Key Topics

The relationship between the Examination side and the Appeals side of the IRS has always been contentious. This tension springs from the different roles each organization has within the Service.

The Examination side has the role of identifying tax problems in the tax return, analyzing the proper tax treatment for these problems, calculating a new tax, including interest and penalties, and then proposing adjustments to the taxpayer's return. If the taxpayer agrees, the tax, including appropriate interest and penalties, will be paid and the issue closed.

If the taxpayer disagrees with the proposed tax treatment, his recourse is to petition the Appeals side for relief. The role of Appeals is to look at the issues brought up by the Examination side and make a determination, based on the likelihood of winning the case in court, should the issue be litigated. The Appeals side, by its nature, usually asks for less tax from the taxpayer than the Examination side because of litigation hazards.

IRS examiners do not like to see a case go to Appeals. They will have invested many hours in the examination and will be convinced that the issues raised and the proposed increases in tax are appropriate. It is disturbing to them when the Appeals side upsets their findings.

It was with this backdrop that I entered the Large and Mid-Size Business Division (LMSB) in April of 2001. It is important to note that LMSB handles only the examination side.

I quickly found out that many agents in LMSB were distrustful of Appeals. However, I learned that many agents in Appeals did not think much of LMSB either.

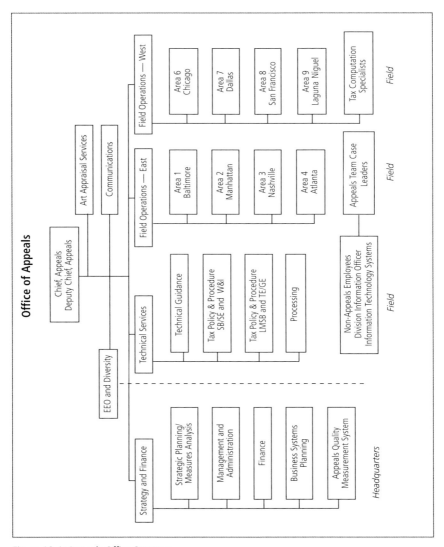

Figure 12-1: Appeals Office Structure.

Appeals and the IRS Restructuring and Reform Act of 1998

I was amazed that two divisions of the IRS could be so far apart on their analysis and disposition of corporate tax issues. The reason for this divide, I discovered, can be traced in great part to two provisions in the IRS Restructuring and Reform Act of 1998.

One of the provisions of the Act required the IRS to establish an independent Office of Appeals. This office was to be accorded the freedom to make decisions on appeals from taxpayers regardless of the dictates of the Examination side.

Another provision concerns *ex parte* communications, a Latin expression that refers to communications that take place in the absence of one of the parties — specifically the taxpayer or the taxpayer's representative.

This provision prohibits communications between the Examination side and the Appeals side on matters of substance, unless the taxpayer has approved of the communication. Communications between the Examination side and the Appeals side are not forbidden by this provision if the communications involve procedural, administrative or ministerial matters.

The purpose of the *ex parte* legislation was to ensure the independence of the Appeals organization. It helped make certain that Appeals would not be influenced by the Examination side over substantive matters, but instead could make its own independent assessment of the correct tax.

For example, discussion of a substantive issue about whether an item qualified for the Research and Experimental Tax Credit would not be allowed while a procedural matter as to the timing of the appeal would be appropriate for the two sides to discuss.

One major exception to the *ex parte* substantive rule is when the topic relates to issue discussions involving a large group of taxpayers or an industry.

For example, if the Research and Experimental Tax Credit issue involved a large group of similarly situated taxpayers or an industry grouping, such as the software industry, it would be permissible for the Examination side and the Appeals side to discuss the best ways to handle the issue to ensure the correct tax result and to be fair to all taxpayers. Based on these discussions of the issue, the Appeals side may reach its own independent decision that the hazards of litigation favor the taxpayer one-third of the time and the IRS two-thirds of the time and may be willing to write Appeals Settlement Guidelines to this effect.

The IRS struggled for about two years before it finally decided that this *ex parte* exception existed. Once decided upon, the Examination side and the Appeals side began to have more collaborative relations over the best way to treat issues.

Appeals Settlement Guidelines

Recently, the Examination side has been encouraging the Appeals side to issue more Appeals Settlement Guidelines. I have noticed many more Appeals Settlement Guidelines issued in the past few years. This is a very helpful way to improve relations between Examinations and Appeals. If the examiners find that Appeals has issued Appeals Settlement Guidelines for an issue, they can settle on this basis and avoid having the case go to Appeals.

Agents on the Examination side are also doing a more effective job of preparing their issues before they go to Appeals. This can be attributed to a strong education effort within the LMSB organization and reviews by LMSB issue-specialist technical advisors and division counsel before the issues are presented. The result is that the positions of the Examination side are more credible to Appeals, and they are more frequently upheld.

Much credit for the improvement in relations between Examinations and Appeals must be given to the hard work of the Chief, Appeals and Deputy Chief, Appeals and to the LMSB leadership team. While the occasional hard feelings are to be expected when Appeals overturns the findings of the Examination side, tensions between the two sides have eased.

The Improving Relationship Between Examination and Appeals

Over the past two years some members of the LMSB top management team have transferred to the Appeals team, a blending of personnel that has brought to Appeals a better understanding of the mission and needs of LMSB, and thus helped to improve communications. In addition, several new initiatives have been implemented that are designed to save taxpayers and the Service a considerable amount of resource time and money. These initiatives come under the heading of alternative dispute resolution procedures.

In contrast to the normal appeals procedure where the taxpayer first petitions Appeals for a hearing, gets the hearing on the calendar, and then consumes months if not years in the process, these new procedures are designed to accelerate the appeals time frame and also save the taxpayer money.

Fast Track Settlement Procedure

The most important new initiative is the Fast Track Settlement Procedure. This program is jointly administered by the Examination side and the Appeals side. The Fast Track Settlement Procedure allows LMSB personnel and LMSB taxpayers an opportunity to mediate their disputes with the help of an Appeals Official acting as a neutral party. LMSB retains jurisdiction over the case. Sometimes the Appeals Official may also recommend a settlement based on his analysis of the issues.

The Fast Track Settlement Procedure is optional for the taxpayer. It does not eliminate or replace existing dispute resolution options, including the taxpayer's opportunity to request a hearing before Appeals. The goal is to promote resolution within 120 days of acceptance into the program.

If the taxpayer decides to try the Fast Track process, he must be fully prepared to present his issues and must be accompanied by decision makers who have the authority to bind his company in resolving the issues. The same is true for the Service. They will need the appropriate decision makers in the room.

Not all cases will be eligible for this procedure. For example, Fast Track does not apply to issues in a taxpayer's case that are considered for litigation, or ones that have been so designated, or for issues outside LMSB's jurisdiction.

The prohibition against *ex parte* communications between the Appeals Officer and the Examination side does not apply to communications arising in a Fast Track Settlement Procedure. This results because Appeals personnel, in facilitating an agreement between the taxpayer and LMSB, are not acting in their traditional Appeals settlement role and are performing their function while the case is still on the Examination side.

Taxpayers tell me they like Fast Track Settlement Procedures because the Appeals time is generally reduced from several years to a few months. In addition, the cost of outside professional help in the preparation of briefs is less, and a quicker timeframe reduces interest expense.

About 85% of cases going into Fast Track Settlement are resolved. This number is about the same as the percentage for cases going through the longer, more arduous appeals process. Early data show that the average fast track case is resolved in about 80 days — well within Appeal's target goal of 120 days.

The Fast Track Settlement Procedure now receives about a quarter of the cases going into Appeals, and I predict this number will grow significantly in the future because of the savings in time and interest expense.

Fast Track Mediation

Fast Track Mediation is an alternative dispute resolution procedure initiative that was recently proposed by the IRS to expedite case resolution. The mediation session, which may be initiated at the conclusion of an examination, is designed to help facilitate communication between the taxpayer and the examination team and help resolve issues upon which they could not agree.

In the Fast Track Mediation process, the taxpayer and the examination team meet with an Appeals Officer who has been trained in mediation. Stringent schedules are applied in order to provide taxpayers a more timely resolution of tax disputes. The entire process is to be completed within 30–40 days. During this process the case will remain within the jurisdiction of LMSB.

I think the jury is still out on Fast Track Mediation. While it appears to be a good tool, I believe most taxpayers are heading in the direction of Fast Track Settlement.

Aside from these new alternative dispute resolution tools, taxpayers should not forget the other tools mentioned in Chapter Seven. These relate to Delegation Order 236, Delegation Order 4-25 (formerly Delegation Order 247) and the procedure of early referral to appeals.

Delegation Orders 236 and 4-25

To refresh your memory, Delegation Order 236 gives the LMSB team manager the authority to settle an issue with the taxpayer where Appeals has previously settled the same issue of the taxpayer in an earlier audit. Delegation 4-25 gives the LMSB team manager the authority to settle an issue with the taxpayer based on issued Appeals Settlement Guidelines.

Early Referral to Appeals

The procedure of early referral to Appeals has some merit if it is commenced early on in the examination cycle. As cases are closed more quickly, however, fewer early referrals to Appeals will be made. Instead, the taxpayer may want to use the Fast Track Settlement Procedure as a way of completing the appeal within the time limits of the audit.

Chapter 13

Advocacy Before the IRS

Key Topics

During my four years with the Large and Mid-Size Business Division (LMSB), a number of companies were successful in working with LMSB for audit guidance and simplification.

The senior leadership of LMSB, led first by Commissioner Larry Langdon and then by his successor, Commissioner Debbie Nolan, have worked hard to stay in touch with taxpayers and to listen to their concerns about current and proposed regulations, rulings and other forms of guidance.

Large taxpayer organizations, such as the Tax Executives Institute (TEI), the American Institute of Certified Public Accountants (AICPA), and the American Bar Association (ABA), stay in touch with the senior LMSB leadership on a regular basis and engage this leadership continually on IRS policies and procedures.

These organizations also serve as sounding boards to the LMSB leadership for new proposals. For example, they have been actively engaged in the design of taxpayer burden reduction programs, the Schedule M-3 to the Form 1120, and corporate e-file.

Other smaller organizations, such as trade associations, also have been active in making their views known to the LMSB leadership. Prominent among these organizations have been the American Electronics Association, the Motion Picture Association of America, and the Broadband Institute.

While trade associations have good access to the LMSB commissioner, they typically spend more of their time engaging in discussions of tax policies and procedures with the industry directors of their respective industries.

Individual company taxpayers also have access to the top LMSB leadership. Oftentimes an issue will arise out of an audit where the taxpayer feels attention at a higher level is needed. While the commissioner may be open to a hearing, it generally is better not to go above the industry director level because those at the industry level are usually better able to understand the individual company's issues.

Industry Advocacy

An excellent forum for industry advocacy is at TEI, AICPA, ABA or trade association events where taxpayers sit on speaking panels with IRS senior leaders. Here is an opportunity for industry to present to the IRS leadership a well-reasoned, powerful discourse on the need for or against a certain tax policy or procedure. It is of the utmost importance to be professional in your comments. *Do not play the blame game against IRS individuals.* It is perfectly appropriate, however, to bring in such concepts as burden reduction, taxpayer equity, complexity and international competitiveness.

Company Advocacy

I recommend that you jump at the chance to be invited to IRS subindustry meetings. These meetings are usually held annually for a specific subindustry of a major industry grouping. For example, the Communications, Technology and Media Group holds an annual high-technology hardware meeting. Revenue agents from around the country convene to share best-practices knowledge of high-technology tax issues and the best ways to handle these issues on audit.

The industry director often invites a few industry representatives to the meeting to share their perspectives of audit practices and tax policies with the agents. If you are invited to attend, you have a chance to influence the thinking of a large body of key IRS personnel and senior leadership working in your industry. Be well prepared and professional. If necessary, coordinate with others in your industry about the message you want to convey.

What will come of all of this hard advocacy effort?

Sometimes nothing at all.

There are also stories where taxpayers have come to a satisfactory resolution of their issues.

Typically two types of taxpayer resolutions have been achieved from these industry presentations: the industry issue resolution agreement and the industry director's directive.

Industry Issue Resolution (IIR) Agreement

This type of resolution is more fully described in Chapter Seven. Many industries in LMSB have used it to take a contentious factual issue off the table and, in essence, create, through a revenue ruling or revenue procedure, a safe harbor tax methodology to be used by taxpayers that will not be challenged on audit.

The broadband industry succeeded in getting an IIR after making a persuasive case at an IRS subindustry meeting that such an agreement was necessary in the area of one way-two way cable depreciation. Other IIRs were issued to the golf course industry relating to the depreciation of golf course greens and to the movie industry relating to the treatment of the year of deductibility of abandoned movie and TV scripts.

Industry Director Directive (IDD)

Sometimes an IDD, a directive issued by the Industry Director, will augment an IIR. For example, an IDD augmented the golf course greens' IIR by stating that tees, sand traps, and fairways could also be subject to depreciation.

More often, I have seen IDDs used as a way to limit the use of IRS resources to an issue. IDDs have been issued for the gaming and restaurant industries relating to the depreciation periods of various components of buildings and equipment.

The sports industry had a contentious issue regarding what part of a sports team acquisition related to deductible tangible assets and what part related to nondeductible intangible assets. An IDD solved this contentious issue by giving the taxpayer certainty that the Service would not challenge transactions where 60% or less of the assets were treated as tangible. In the 2004 tax bill, the intangibles issue was resolved by letting taxpayers write off intangibles from sports franchise acquisitions over 15 years.

Other areas where the IDD may be useful include the Research and Experimental Tax Credit area and the mergers and acquisitions area involving deductible versus nondeductible transaction expenses. Both of these areas are extremely resource intensive for the Service. If the Service could use more industry director directives, it would free up agents to complete the audit more quickly and move on to other audits.

Chapter 14

IRS ALTERNATIVE — ADVOCACY BEFORE THE CONGRESS

Key Topics

I spent the first half of my career as a tax lawyer employed by Fortune 500 companies. Like many of my colleagues in the corporate tax world, I endeavored to understand the tax code and the regulations, rulings, case law and other forms of tax guidance. I often complained about the inequity of certain tax regulations or rulings, or about audit positions taken by the IRS. But, like many others in my position, I only complained and never did anything to remedy the problem.

I spent the second half of my career with a Fortune 500 company, but was not involved directly in corporate tax department work. Instead, I worked with the U.S. Congress and legislatures of California and Texas. A substantial part of this effort was to help pass tax laws to benefit the high-technology sector.

From my legislative experience I learned that if you do not like a tax provision, whether tax law, regulation, ruling, case law, or IRS audit position, stop complaining and get the law changed. It's not easy getting a law changed, but with hard work, patience and perseverance, it can often be accomplished.

Considering the Legislative Route

When considering the legislative route, you should review the equity of your position and the tax savings involved for your company and your industry. The stronger your equity argument the easier it will be to accomplish change.

Success in passing a bill with a light equity argument but large potential tax savings is not impossible, but it will take longer and involve more resources — with no assurance that you will be able to accomplish your desired result.

An issue with a light equity argument and small tax savings usually should not be attempted. The chances are slim that you will get your legislation passed and the cost to your company and industry might exceed the hoped-for tax savings.

In deciding on the legislative route, there are additional factors to consider. These include the timing of the introduction of the legislation, the political make-up of the U.S. Congress, the political make-up of the White House and the U.S. Treasury Department, and the disposition of the IRS towards your issue.

Timing is Everything

Timing is everything. I believe in the mood-of-the-country theory. When the mood is friendly towards your issue, strike while the iron is hot. Introduce legislation immediately.

An example of this theory is the period after the tsunami that struck South Asia on December 26, 2004. Millions of dollars of charitable contributions were needed from private donors to aid tsunami victims. Within a few days, Congress passed legislation that the president signed extending to January 31, 2005 the time period for charitable contributions that could be claimed on the individual's 2004 Form 1040.

The political make-up of the U.S. Congress is very important. Do you have a Congress in power that you think will be supportive of your issue? If the Congress is philosophically supportive, are they willing to make your issue a priority? Do you have key members of the Ways and Means Committee and Senate Finance Committee who will make this a priority issue? Is there room in the overall congressional budget to accommodate your legislative request?

If your goal is, for example, to reduce the taxation of capital gains, you might have a better chance of success if a Republican rather than a Democratic Congress is in power. Republicans have historically championed a low capital gains rate and the Democrats have opposed a low rate.

The political make-up of the White House and the Treasury Department are very important. A White House with a goal of budget reductions may not look favorably on new tax legislation that increases the budget. The Bush Treasury Department has been interested in tax policy proposals that help improve international competitiveness for U.S. companies. If your proposal falls within their roadmap, you will have a better chance of Treasury Department support and ultimate success.

Then there is the IRS factor. Congress will consult the IRS with regard to your proposal. Their input to the Congress can be damaging or it can be helpful. They may be neutral or even like your proposal, but they may have to administer the law in a way you do not like. They can help you by not opposing your proposal.

Introducing Your Bill

Once you think all of the signs are right, that is, your issue has a strong equity basis, a sizeable dollar impact, the right timing, a favorable Congress and Administration, and hopefully an IRS that will not damage your case, what are the next steps?

1. *You will want members of the Congress on both sides of the aisle to introduce your bill.* Ideally, you will have members of both the House and Senate introduce this bill at about the same time. Having as co-authors several members of the House Ways and Means Committee and the Senate Finance Committee can be helpful in influencing their respective committee members of the merits of the bill and aiding in getting it passed out of committee.

2. *Line up other House and Senate members* to sign on to your bill as co-sponsors. This indicates broader congressional support for your proposal.

3. *Prepare an accurate and honest analysis of the cost* of your bill over a five- and ten-year period. Economists who specialize in this type of analysis can work with your data. This analysis is important to build congressional support and increase overall chances of success.

4. *Prepare succinct one- and two-page analyses* of your bill showing the benefits it can provide to your industry, to the employment picture, international competitiveness or some other important national interest.

5. *Have patience.* You may not be successful in getting your issue passed the first year or even in five years.

6. *Persevere.* Do not give up. Having a legislative success is like catching the one-thousand-pound marlin. You can only do it on a few occa-

sions, if at all. You may need to keep this issue in front of the members of Congress for many years. Keep educating them about the benefits of your bill. If your bill has merit, it is likely to pass eventually.

7. *Do not hesitate to move beyond the Congress* in building support for your bill. Talk to newspaper editorial boards about the merits of your issue. Submit op-ed pieces to selected newspapers and magazines. If possible, build support with the unions.

8. *Engage in the political process.* One of the most important concerns for a politician is getting re-elected. Contribute to supporters of your bill through donations at their fundraisers.

Reward for a Job Well Done

After all of your hard advocacy work, your patience and your perseverance, what might be your reward?

The Job Creation Act of 2004 is an example of legislation that provided a positive answer to many corporate taxpayers in the form of significant tax relief.

A number of manufacturing companies with offshore operations received a grace period during 2004–2005 in order to bring back to the U.S. untaxed overseas profits at a 5.25% tax rate versus the normal 35% corporate tax rate.

The motion picture industry got a long-sought change in the computation of depreciation by the income forecast method, which, on a retroactive basis, saved them millions of tax dollars.

The sports industry got to amortize intangibles on the purchase of sports franchises over fifteen years. Prior to this change, such intangibles had to be capitalized and no part was amortizable.

NASCAR, fighting an attempt by the IRS to require a fifteen-year life for the depreciation of race track facilities, mobilized the Congress and succeeded in obtaining a seven-year life.

Not every year will have legislation for companies as favorable as the Job Creation Act of 2004. This legislation did not happen overnight, however.

The Act contained many bills that had been in existence in the Congress for many years. The sponsors of these bills continued to advocate for them with many different constituencies. Finally, the timing for passage was right. The bills were collected into final Ways and Means and Senate Finance Committee versions, resolved through a Joint House-Senate Committee Conference, and then signed by the president. This just shows that patience and perseverance can pay off.

Chapter 15

CHARTING THE FUTURE OF THE LARGE AND MID-SIZE BUSINESS DIVISION

Key Topics

As I stated in Chapter Four, I had four major goals that I wanted to accomplish within the Large and Mid-Size Business Division (LMSB):

1. *Improve relations between industry and the IRS.*

2. *Reduce the audit time and cost burden for industry and the IRS.*

3. *Help U.S. industry become more competitive.*

4. *Introduce private industry efficiency to the IRS.*

Improving Relations Between Industry and the IRS

I have always taken the position that a good relationship between members of a corporate tax department and its IRS auditors will pay dividends to the corporation through a shorter audit, less interest expense, fewer potential proposed penalties, and more instances where the company is given the benefit of the doubt on nebulous issues.

When corporate tax executives treat IRS auditors with respect, respect often is returned. That was my experience in the corporate tax community. Agents would often give me the benefit of the doubt on issues because I had established a relationship of trust and rapport with them.

At LMSB, however, I heard agents complain that they had been treated poorly by the corporate team. They were misled as to the facts of various transactions, put in bad working conditions at the corporate site, and generally treated in a hostile manner.

Such disrespect toward agents is bound to cause resentment. Where once they might have been willing to give the taxpayer the benefit of the doubt on an issue, now they are digging in and are being resistant to any proposed leeway.

In my position as Senior Industry Advisor, I was determined to break down barriers between agents and companies. At least once a year I organized an industry/IRS dinner at my house. The goal was to bring the two sides together and let them discuss topics other than taxes. I wanted them to develop relationships that might carry over if they ever met later in an audit.

I encouraged the Tax Executives Institute to provide opportunities for IRS senior executives to meet their membership. I invited industry executives to attend IRS meetings for discussions of important industry issues and joint explorations of ways to improve tax administration.

The seventh grade dance environment that I alluded to in my introductory chapter has improved. The IRS team and the industry team no longer stand on opposite sides of the room. They congregate, sit together at the same table, and carry on cordial conversation.

As a result, I feel good about this agenda item. I think I made some difference here.

Reducing the Audit Time and Cost Burden for Industry and the IRS

When I first joined LMSB, the excessive time required for corporate audits was a common topic for discussion. On average, these audits were lasting at least 60 months. Some were still unresolved after ten to fifteen years.

I learned that a single segment of the audit cycle could take up to a year or more. This segment began with the receipt of returns from the corporate taxpayer and included the entry of this information into the statistics of income system, after which a copy was made available for review and possible audit. Agents in the field complained that they were being asked to audit returns two and three years after they had been filed.

In 2004, the IRS instituted a scanning program. All corporate returns are now scanned at the IRS Service Center in Ogden, Utah, after which the original is sent to the statistics of income group and a copy is made available for possible audit. This simple procedure appears to have shaved about 12 months from the audit cycle.

Lengthy response times for information document requests (IDRs) had always been a prime topic for discussion at IRS management meetings. Companies are now beginning to respond more quickly for a combination of reasons. First of all, taxpayers and the IRS are taking the time to discuss the purpose and scope of the IDR beforehand, and this results in an IDR request that is easier for the taxpayer to understand. Secondly, taxpayers are becoming more aware that a long audit is not good for their company as interest on a tax deficiency will continue to accrue on a daily basis and shareholders are left in limbo as to the true financial state of their company involved in a tax audit.

LMSB Commissioners Larry Langdon and Debbie Nolan implemented many taxpayer-friendly initiatives that have saved time and money for corporate taxpayers. A few of these time-savers are enumerated in Chapter Seven. I have been especially pleased to see how well some of them are working.

My favorite taxpayer-friendly initiative is the Fast Track Settlement Procedure, which is described in Chapters Seven and Twelve. Both taxpayers and the IRS like the time- and cost-saving benefits of this initiative. Normal appeal times have dropped from several years to an average of 80–120 days. I think taxpayers will continue to embrace this initiative, and I predict that over half of the corporate appeals will be handled this way over the next five years.

My next favorite is the Industry Director's Directive. I describe it more fully in Chapter Thirteen. This initiative essentially permits an industry director to request the agents in his directorate not to audit transactions that fall within certain benchmark guidelines. The purpose of the directive is to save IRS resources that can be used for other issues or company audits.

I also like the concept of pre-filing agreements (PFAs). Unfortunately very few PFAs have been approved for taxpayer use due to IRS resource constraints. Some have been used in the Research and Experimental Tax Credit area, some for valuations of assets, and some for mergers and acquisitions.

I believe that PFAs are under-used with regard to acquisitions. A PFA allows the acquiring company to work with the target company to engage in a tax audit of the acquisition. Initiated shortly after the acquisition, a PFA can be valuable because the target company's personnel and records are usually still available. At a later time, company records may have disappeared and employees who knew about the transaction may no longer be on staff.

An initiative that I predict will gain legs over the next ten years is the Compliance Assurance Process (CAP). It is a procedure that completely revolutionizes the way corporate tax returns are prepared and filed. Rather than filing a return 9 1/2 months after its year end, including extensions, corporations will now be able to file a return shortly after the end of their accounting year, with the assurance that the items on the return have met IRS scrutiny and have been approved.

The CAP process will require a close working relationship between the taxpayer and the IRS during the company's financial year. Typically, the company and the IRS will try to identify the key items they want to look at during the year and resolve these items, either in favor of the taxpayer or the IRS. The full arsenal of IRS tools, including PFAs and the Fast Track Settlement Procedure, could be available to help resolve difficult issues. Unresolved issues (and hopefully there will be just a few) may go on to Appeals or to court. The remaining issues will receive IRS approval and the return will be treated as final.

To date, only companies with an outstanding history of good tax compliance, a lack of abusive tax shelters, and the ability to work cooperatively with the IRS have been selected into the CAP program.

The CEOs of the companies selected for the CAP program embrace it because of the prestige focused on their participation. These companies will get the benefit of publicizing this selection in their promotional literature, in their annual government filings, and elsewhere that they have been selected in the CAP program because they have exhibited highly ethical behavior in the preparation of their taxes and in their interactions with the IRS.

CEOs of other companies will, undoubtedly, want to achieve CAP status too, and will support their CFOs and tax directors in bringing their tax compliance functions to a level that will qualify in the future.

In a sense, selection into the CAP program could be analogous to selection for the prestigious Malcolm Baldridge Quality Award. We shall see if history proves me right on this point.

I applaud the efforts of the LMSB leadership team to reduce the audit time and cost burden for industry and the IRS. Kudos to those who designed the concepts of fast track appeals, industry director directives, pre-filing agreements, and CAP. I am also proud to have been a part of this process.

Helping U.S. Industry Become More Competitive

Before I joined the IRS, a substantial part of my career had been dedicated to helping U.S. industry become more competitive. I had worked hard with my industry colleagues to break down foreign trade barriers, to stop injurious foreign dumping of goods, to protect the intellectual property rights of U.S. companies, and to promote sound federal and state tax policies that put our companies on an even footing with foreign competitors.

When I discussed these concerns within the IRS, the staffers were either uncomprehending or they would claim that U.S. companies can take care of themselves. Most usually they would say their job was to apply the law and IRS regulations and not to think about U.S. competitiveness.

In some cases, the IRS will draft regulations that would satisfy a purist but be totally out of sync with international realities. Oftentimes, the IRS will have the discretion to make the right choice from an international competitiveness standpoint, but will instead choose to apply the "correct" tax answer.

During my term I had the privilege to work with Mark Weinberger and Pamela Olson, successive Assistant Secretaries of the Treasury for Tax Policy in the Treasury Department. I applaud their pro-competitive speeches and actions. These stances were music to my ears. I believe the tax community also applauds them, particularly as they relate to the U.S. taxation of foreign income of U.S. companies.

My compatriots at the IRS, however, treat Treasury as its own separate entity apart from their organization, often sneering at Treasury Department competitiveness proposals. This is not productive.

Weinberger and Olson have now left the government. Weinberger joined the accounting firm of Ernst & Young and Olson joined the law firm of Skadden, Arps, Slate, Meagher & Flom.

While governments in other countries support private industry or at least remain neutral on their behalf, it is common for the IRS to view U.S. industry with distrust instead of appreciating it for the job producer that it is. We tend to bog down U.S. companies doing business internationally with expensive and complex audits that their foreign counterparts do not have.

I think it is important to remember that tax policy is trade policy; trade policy is tax policy; they should go down the same road and in the same direction. In this context, Treasury and the IRS should try to go down the same road and in the same direction. If the Secretary of the Treasury can align the views of the IRS and the Treasury Department's Tax Policy side in the area of international competitiveness, it will be a noble achievement for the country.

A new law that I believe is causing problems of crisis proportions for U.S. businesses is the 2002 Sarbanes-Oxley Act. The law requires public companies to prove that they have strong internal control systems to detect employee wrongdoing and prevent accounting errors before financial statements are made public. The hardships on financial and tax activities imposed by this legislation affect our ability to compete in international markets. In my role as Senior Industry Advisor, I heard from many companies, particularly in the high-tech sector, about the costs of Sarbanes-Oxley compliance.

One semiconductor company CEO with one hundred million dollars in sales voiced concern that he was spending one million dollars a year on Sarbanes-Oxley compliance, money that could be used to hire engineers to design and build new products.

Companies in the one billion dollar sales range commonly pay about five million dollars a year for compliance. Larger companies pay much more. One board member of a high-tech company told me his firm spends about one-half of each board meeting discussing Sarbanes-Oxley issues, time that would otherwise be spent on company strategic discussions.

A significant portion of this cost goes toward insuring appropriate tax compliance. Tax directors have informed me that Sarbanes-Oxley has caused them to be concerned about the potential for having to restate company financials over tax issues where there is no clear answer. This confusion is often the result of new legislation, such as the Jobs Creation Act of 2004, where companies had to make corporate tax decisions within a short time frame, with little regulatory guidance as to the correct tax answer.

Although the legislation is well-intentioned, many business experts think that Sarbanes-Oxley would have failed to identify the criminal activities at Enron and WorldCom. At the same time, it has engendered a substantial compliance and cost burden for U.S. companies. It may be time to begin thinking about softening the edges of Sarbanes-Oxley, first by examining where it causes the greatest compliance problems for companies, and then, where necessary, by making corrective legislative changes to reduce the cost burden. This law is draining so much cash out of the corporate sector in compliance costs that it is one of the reasons U.S. job growth is so lackluster.

Introducing Private Industry Efficiency to the IRS

I am constantly amazed at how many individuals and departments at the IRS get involved in handling the simplest matters. Regrettably, this appears to be the way government works at most federal agencies.

> ➢ There are too many sign-off procedures.
> ➢ There are too many rules.
> ➢ There are too many penalties for breaking the rules.

While it is true that government has to have safeguards to protect the public interest, the problem is that safeguards keep being added to other safeguards with no end in sight. People in government get used to Byzantine rules and exceptions, and some employees make careers out of knowing them. They are complex and they waste millions of hours of time. This type of waste is not in the public's best interest. In the IRS, a significant portion of its budget goes toward these wasteful activities.

I have already noted that there is an apparent lack of sympathy in the system for the value of a government employee's time. For example, if you need to travel from your hotel to a crosstown meeting in Washington DC that would take five minutes by cab, ten minutes by rapid transit, and thirty minutes by bus, government policy would suggest that you take the bus if that were the least expensive mode of transportation.

I have also commented on meetings full of people with only a few contributing and of meetings lasting too many days with nothing to do.

One of my goals was to improve efficiency in the overall operation of the IRS. Like many other corporate executives who entered into government service with the best of intentions, this is an area about which I made little headway.

I believe one answer is to continue to look for more ways to get the job done without adding resources. In the private sector, this was a priority. The government sector has not always been forced to do so, which has resulted in the addition of ever more bureaucratic rules to fill up staff hours in the work day.

In the private sector, companies can lay off workers in order to reduce budgets. In government, it is almost impossible to reduce staff. The National Treasury Employees Union, which represents IRS employees, is a strong foe to any staff reductions. Clearly, there are areas in the IRS bureaucracy where people have little to do. Still, IRS keeps increasing its budget dollar requests to the Congress.

My advice to those private sector employees following me into government is to keep on trying to improve government efficiency. I do believe some of my efforts helped. Hopefully yours will also.

Charting New Directions for LMSB

Corporate taxpayers should be aware that LMSB is beginning to broaden its audit scope to new areas and to more companies.

> ➢ One new focus area is executive compensation. Spot checks of this area by LMSB executive compensation teams have indicated some compliance issues. There are even stories of some top executives who have failed to file individual tax returns. If I were a corporate tax director, I would have an independent accounting or law firm

review all of my company's executive compensation plans and modify them, if necessary, to bring them into IRS compliance.

➢ More company executive tax shelter arrangements are coming under scrutiny as abusive tax avoidance schemes, and I would look closely at the wisdom of keeping them.

➢ New emphasis will be placed on overseas transfer pricing issues, especially in the area of parent-subsidiary cost sharing arrangements for the high-technology sector. The Service is convinced there is a potential problem and will be focusing on this area through various forms of guidance, court contests and possibly legislation.

➢ The IRS plans to audit more companies. A 2005 survey by the Tax Executives Institute reported that only about 44% of companies that responded to the survey were undergoing IRS audits. The survey companies included about one-half of the Fortune 1000 and about one-half of the Tax Executives Institute membership. These companies presumably were all LMSB companies.

The goal of the IRS is to spend less time auditing the largest taxpayers and to put more of its resources toward the middle and smaller of the LMSB taxpayers. Thus, middle and smaller companies that have avoided audits in the past should prepare for the day when they too may be examined. The new Schedule M-3 to the Form 1120 and corporate e-file will help screen potential middle and smaller companies for audit.

Considering the accomplishments of LMSB thus far, and the direction in which it is headed, I believe LMSB will continue as a very efficient and effective tax agency for the U.S. government. I extend to LMSB employees and management my sincerest best wishes.

Index

Numerics

401(k) plans 34

A

abandoned movie and TV scripts 73, 125
abusive tax avoidance shelters 27, 74, 77, 145
   reducing caseload 84
   structured as trusts or partnerships 84
academia 15
Accelerated Issue Resolution (AIR) Agreements 71, 82, 90
acronymophobia 40
acronyms 40
Adams, Bob 22
Advanced Micro Devices (AMD) 1, 31, 87
advocacy before IRS 121–126
advocacy before the Congress 127–133
affordable housing 50
Agilent Technologies 4
aging of LMSB workforce 83
Alcoa Corporation 21
Alcohol Tobacco Tax and Trade Bureau 96
American Bar Association (ABA) 5, 87, 90, 123
American Electronics Association 123
American Institute of Certified Public Accountants (AICPA) 5, 87, 90, 123
Appeals 84, 92
   early referral to 119
   Fast Track Appeals 74
   IRS 113, 115–118
   Officers 84
   Settlement Guidelines 116
Area Counsels 107

Assistant Secretary (Tax Policy) 65, 96, 97
audit cycle 138
audits
   cycle time 77
   effect of Industry Director's Directives (IDDs) 125
   frequency of 82
   increasing "survival-ability" 9
   Joint Audit Planning Process 75
   length of time 81
   of IRS employees 34, 63
   reducing cost burden for industry 138
   reducing time 65, 81, 138

B

bad debt issues 73
Bank of America 1
Berg, Doug 22
Beyond High Tech Survival — Turning Government Policy into International Profits 2
Big Brother 42
BP 22
Brazzil, Bob 20
broadband industry 125
Broadband Institute 123
budget year 61
budgets
   federal government agency 96
   IRS 96
   IRS vs. industry 61
   Treasury Department 96
Bureau of Engraving and Printing 96
Burke, Linda 4, 8, 25
Business Systems Planning (LMSB) 24

C

cable industry 90
California Bar Association 1

J

N

NASCAR 132

National Treasury Employees Union (NTEU) 59, 144

Natural Resources and Construction group (LMSB) 20

New York University School of Law 1

newspaper editorial boards 132

Ng, Frank 8, 21, 26

Nolan, Deborah 4, 20, 21, 25, 26, 27, 41, 123, 139

Nortel Networks 22

O

O'Malley, Jim 7, 21

Office of Appeals organization chart 114

Office of Pre-Filing and Technical Guidance 7, 8

Office of Tax Shelter Analysis (OTSA) 7, 27

Office of the Assistant Secretary of the Treasury for Tax Policy 109

Office of the Chief Counsel, organization chart 105

Ogden, Utah Service Center (IRS) 81

Ohio 62

Oklahoma City bombing 58

Olson, Pamela 141

op-ed pieces 132

Organization of Economic Co-operation and Development (OECD) 3

Ottawa, Canada 3

overseas profits 132

overseas transfer pricing 145

Oversight Subcommittee (Ways and Means Committee) 98

overstaffing, IRS vs. industry 63

P

pensions 50

Performance, Quality Assurance, and Audit Assurance (LMSB) 24

Petrella, John 26

political process 132

Pre-Filing Agreements (PFAs) 27, 71, 72, 82, 90, 139

Pre-Filing and Technical Guidance (LMSB) 21

PricewaterhouseCoopers 21

pro-competitive speeches and actions 141

profit sharing 59

publishing industry 90

Q

quality control, LMSB 22

quality-of-life issues, IRS vs. industry 59

R

race track facilities, depreciation of 132

railroad tracks, IIRs 73

Reese, Jerry 8, 21

regional commissioners, IRS 4

Research and Experimental Tax Credit 72, 87, 115, 125, 139

restaurant industry 125

 small ware IIRs 73

Retailers, Food, Pharmaceutical and Healthcare group (LMSB) 20

revenue procedure 73

revenue ruling 73

Robison, Dave 3, 20, 31

Rossotti, Charles 3, 19, 25

Russian KGB 63

OLIVE HILL
LANE PRESS

How to Order

By Fax: Please print and fill out this form, then fax it to (650) 322-5505.

By Telephone: Call toll free (866) 473-1761.
(Please have your AMEX, MasterCard, or VISA ready.)

By Mail: Please print and fill out this form, then mail it to

> Olive Hill Lane Press
> 2995 Woodside Road, Suite 400
> Woodside, CA 94062

Quantity

Please send _____ copies of *Corporate Tax Audit Survival* at $24.95 each.

_____ copies of *Beyond High Tech Survival*
(including 2000 supplement) at $19.95 each.

_____ sets of *Corporate Tax Audit Survival* and
Beyond High Tech Survival (including 2000 supplement)
at $39.95 each.

School and corporate discounts available for orders of 5 or more. Please call (866) 473-1761 for pricing.

Sales Tax

Please add 8.25% for books shipped to California addresses.

Shipping & Handling

$7.00 for the first book or set, and $1.00 for each additional book or set, up to five copies or sets (for orders shipped within the U.S.). Please allow up to five days for shipment.

Payment

☐ Check payable to Olive Hill Lane Press (U.S. funds only).

Credit Card: ☐ AMEX ☐ MasterCard ☐ VISA

Card Number: _____

Signature: _____ Exp. Date: _____

Ship To

Name: _____

Title: _____

Company: _____

Address: _____

_____

City: _____ State: _____ Zip: _____

Telephone: _____

CORPORATE TAX AUDIT SURVIVAL **155**